Publisher
UNICORN BOOKS
F-2/16, Ansari Road, Daryaganj, New Delhi-110002
☎ 011-23275434, 23262683, 23250704 • *Fax:* 011-23257790
E-mail: info@unicornbooks.in • *Website:* www.unicornbooks.in

Branch : Mumbai
23-25, Zaoba Wadi, Thakurdwar, Mumbai-401002
☎ 022-22010941, 022-22053387
E-mail: rapidex@bom5.vsnl.net.in

©: Teacher Created Resources
Published in arrangement with Teacher Created Resources, USA by Unicorn Books Pvt. Ltd.

ISBN : 978-81-7806-384-3

Edition: 2019

Printed at : *Param offsetters, Okhla, New Delhi-110020*

Trailblazer
Winning Edge Series

Mathematics WORKBOOK *for* NTSE & Olympiad

Grade - 6

Author
Sandra Cook, M.A.
Helen Leon, M.A.

Table of Contents

Introduction

It is Wednesday afternoon and the teacher has just announced a math test for Friday. Across the classroom, hearts start to race. Looks of dread appear on the faces of the students. Taking a test can be very stressful. Can you remember a time when you studied very hard and thought you knew everything, but you received the test results and were shocked to see a grade that was much lower than you had expected? What happened? Well, you might have known the material, but there is more to taking a test than just knowing the material. To be successful when taking a test, you must also know test-taking strategies.

Taking tests is not something new, but the number of tests taken by a student and the importance of those tests is. This math problem-solving book focuses on the skills that are prevalent on standardized, multiple-choice tests. This book concentrates on understanding the various types of math problems that may be presented for a particular skill and how to evaluate the problems in order to solve them. From preparing students to recognize tricky questions designed to confuse them, to exercises that emphasize the importance of discriminating necessary facts from unnecessary ones, this book gives students the tools and the experience to enable them to critically analyze and solve grade-level-appropriate math problems.

Students will learn test-taking skills needed to become more confident and efficient test takers. Furthermore, students will gain critical-thinking skills that can be used in many situations throughout their test-taking years and beyond.

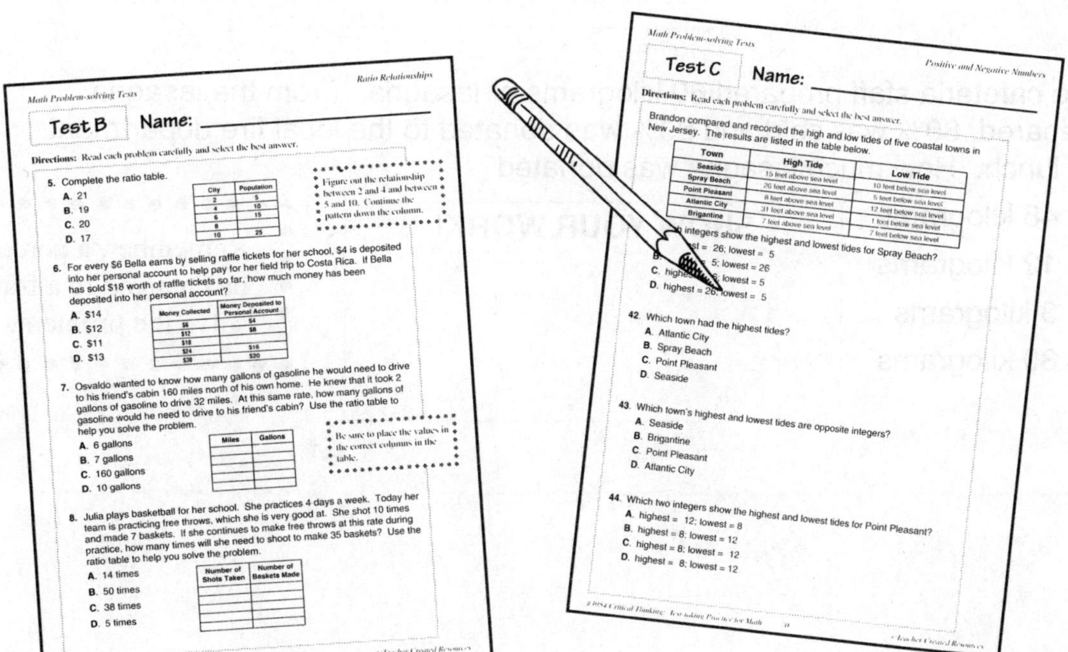

How the Book Is Organized

This book is organized into three tests: Test A, Test B, and Test C. Each test has 100 questions that are aligned to the Common Core State Standards. Different types of questions are included to familiarize students with strategies that are crucial to successful test taking.

There are four questions on each page of the three tests. For continuity, the skill is the same for each question number across all three tests, which means question 14 tests the same skill on Test A as it does on Test B and Test C. These assessments were designed so that the degree of call-out assistance provided decreases from Test A to Test B, with no call-outs on Test C.

Test A

Test A provides students with specific and detailed guidance regarding how to approach each math problem. Call-outs appear as rectangular-shaped boxes that are positioned to the far right of the questions. These call-outs give the students specific information to help solve the problem.

Example from Test A

Directions: Read each problem carefully and select the best answer.

15. Mike will give the waitress a 15% tip. The bill for his dinner is ₹35.40. How much will the waitress receive for a tip?

A. ₹40.71
B. ₹531
C. ₹5.31
D. ₹53.10

SHOW YOUR WORK!

Reread the problem. Did you answer the question that was asked?

16. The cafeteria staff prepared 60 kilograms of lasagna. From the lasagna prepared, 80% was sold and 20% was donated to the local fire department for lunch. How much lasagna was donated?

A. 48 kilograms
B. 12 kilograms
C. 3 kilograms
D. 30 kilograms

SHOW YOUR WORK!

Remember, a percent can be changed to a fraction to solve the problem.

How the Book Is Organized *(cont.)*

Example from Test A *(cont.)*

Test A offers assistance to properly "decode" each question. Work with students throughout this test and encourage critical thinking. Try these strategies:

- Have students underline important facts in order to draw attention to their importance in the solution of the problem.
- Highlight or circle clue words or phrases to help students focus on choosing the correct operation needed to solve the problem.
- Go over the test as a group, reviewing it line by line, to help interpret each problem and each possible answer.

Consider example 16 from Test A. You might underline 60 kilograms, 80% was sold, and 20% was donated. These facts are important to the solution of the problem.

Circle or highlight clues to help you decide what operation to use to solve the problem. In this example, was donated is a clue for subtraction, because the problem is asking how much of the lasagna was given away.

Test B

Test B continues to provide call-out support, but there are fewer call-outs. Test B is another opportunity for students to practice test-taking strategies, such as underlining important facts and highlighting or circling key words and phrases. It offers the teacher a chance to assess which math skills still need additional work.

Example from Test B

Directions: Read each problem carefully and select the best answer.

15. A vote for the Best Artist of the Year was held last week. Ferheena received 65% of the votes. A total of 80 people voted. How many votes did Ferheena receive?

A. 48 votes
B. 52 votes
C. 50 votes
D. 15 votes

SHOW YOUR WORK!

16. Ferheena receives a monthly allowance of ₹200. She plans to use 15% of her allowance to purchase a new scrapbook. How much will the scrapbook cost?

A. ₹3
B. ₹300
C. ₹30
D. ₹12

SHOW YOUR WORK!

Is your answer reasonable?

How the Book Is Organized *(cont.)*

Test C

Test C also provides 100 questions, but no call-out support is provided. It is an opportunity for students to take a math problem-solving assessment independently. This test will give both you and your students an opportunity to see the degree to which they have internalized not only the ability to correctly identify skills needed to solve the problem, but the specific strategies they can employ to answer each question.

Answer Key

The answer key at the back of this book is designed to be another test-taking tool for both teachers and students. Student bubble sheets are also provided on pages 110–112.

While it is important for students to know which answer is correct, it is also useful for students to understand why other options are incorrect. The answer key provides explanations for the correct answers to the questions. Each incorrect answer is also discussed to provide students with possible explanations for why they might have chosen it.

The following example from the answer key shows the answer to one of the questions in the example from Test B on the previous page.

Sample Answer Key Explanation

15. Correct Answer: B

Ferheena received 65% *of* the 80 votes. *Of* means *multiply* and 65% = $\frac{65}{100}$: $\frac{65}{100} \times \frac{80}{1} = \frac{65}{5} \times \frac{4}{1}$ (after cross-cancelling) = $\frac{260}{5}$ = 52.

Incorrect Answers:

A. 60% was used to solve instead of 65%.

C. An error occurred when reducing $\frac{260}{5}$: 260 ÷ 5 ≠ 50.

D. 15 is the difference between 80 and 65 (the two numbers included in the problem).

How to Use the Book

Teachers know that students learn differently. Each class tends to be strong in some skill areas and weak in others. Therefore, it is up to the teacher to decide how to use this book to best benefit the students. Consider the following possibilities:

The book can be completed in the order it has been written. Test A can be completed first, then Test B, and finally Test C. Teachers will lend less support in Test B than in Test A, and Test C can be administered as a true test to assess students' skills.

The book can also be completed in smaller increments, depending on the needs of the class. Since each test has 100 questions, consider dividing the tests into parts. For example, assign problems 1–20 on Test A. Carefully review the questions on this test, along with the call-outs, with the class. Assign the same 20 questions on Test B and review the responses as a group. Finally, assign questions 1–20 on Test C. Test C does not contain any call-outs; students should complete it independently. After completing Test C independently, each question can be reviewed orally and modeled, if necessary, so the students can understand why each answer is correct or incorrect. Any observed weaknesses should be addressed as they arise. Another approach to Test C would be for the teacher to collect and grade the test after students independently complete it. Any areas of weakness should be reviewed and modeled as a class or in a small-group setting.

All answers should be reviewed so students know why an answer was incorrect. Make this an appealing activity by creating a classroom full of detectives. When reviewing answers to the questions, have each student come up with a reason why someone would make that error. For example, the student might state that the problem was wrong because the number facts were added instead of subtracted. Finding the reason for the incorrect answer will help students understand the problem and solve the mystery.

In addition, the tests can be used as study tools. Place the tests and answer sheets in a binder that is accessible to students. They can "self-test" before and between assessments (including standardized tests) to maintain skills and focus on test-taking strategies.

Subject Correlation

Ratios and Proportional Relationships	Problem #s
Understand ratio concepts and use ratio reasoning to solve problems.	
Understand the concept of a ratio and use ratio language to describe a ratio relationship between two quantities.	1–4
Use ratio and rate reasoning to solve real-world and mathematical problems, e.g., by reasoning about tables of equivalent ratios, tape diagrams, double number line diagrams, or equations.	5–8
Make tables of equivalent ratios relating quantities with whole-number measurements, find missing values in the tables, and plot the pairs of values on the coordinate plane. Use tables to compare ratios.	5–8
Solve unit rate problems including those involving unit pricing and constant speed.	9–12
Find a percent of a quantity as a rate per 100 (e.g., 30% of a quantity means 30/100 times the quantity); solve problems involving finding the whole, given a part and the percent.	13–16
The Number System	
Apply and extend previous understandings of multiplication and division to divide fractions by fractions.	
Interpret and compute quotients of fractions, and solve word problems involving division of fractions by fractions.	17–20
Compute fluently with multi-digit numbers and find common factors and multiples.	
Fluently divide multi-digit numbers using the standard algorithm.	21–24
Fluently add, subtract, multiply, and divide multi-digit decimals using the standard algorithm for each operation.	25–28
Find the greatest common factor of two whole numbers less than or equal to 100 and the least common multiple of two whole numbers less than or equal to 12. Use the distributive property to express a sum of two whole numbers 1–100 with a common factor as a multiple of a sum of two whole numbers with no common factor.	29–32, 33–36, 37–40
Apply and extend previous understanding of numbers to the system of rational numbers.	
Understand that positive and negative numbers are used together to describe quantities having opposite directions or values; use positive and negative numbers to represent quantities in real-world contexts, explaining the meaning of 0 in each situation.	41–44
Recognize opposite signs of numbers as indicating locations on opposite sides of 0 on the number line; recognize that the opposite of the opposite of a number is the number itself.	45–48
Understand signs of numbers in ordered pairs as indicating locations in quadrants of the coordinate plane; recognize that when two ordered pairs differ only by signs, the locations of the points are related by reflections across one or both axes.	49–52
Find and position integers and other rational numbers on a horizontal or vertical number line diagram; find and position pairs of integers and other rational numbers on a coordinate plane.	53–56

The Number System *(cont.)*	Problem #s
Apply and extend previous understanding of number to the system of rational numbers. *(cont.)*	
Understand ordering and absolute value of rational numbers.	57–60
Understand the absolute value of a rational number as its distance from 0 on the number line; interpret absolute value as magnitude for a positive or negative quantity in a real-world situation.	61–64
Expressions and Equations	
Apply and extend previous understandings of arithmetic to algebraic expressions.	
Write and evaluate numerical expressions involving whole-number exponents.	65–68
Write, read, and evaluate expressions in which letters stand for numbers.	69–76
Write expressions that record operations with numbers and with letters standing for numbers.	69–72
Evaluate expressions at specific values of their variables. Include expressions that arise from formulas used in real-world problems. Perform arithmetic operations, including those involving whole-number exponents, in the conventional order when there are no parentheses to specify a particular order (Order of Operations).	73–76
Apply the properties of operations to generate equivalent expressions.	77–80
Reason about and solve one-variable equations and inequalities.	
Understand solving an equation or inequality as a process of answering a question: which values from a specified set, if any, make the equation or inequality true? Use substitution to determine whether a given number in a specified set makes an equation or inequality true.	81–84
Geometry	
Solve real-world and mathematical problems involving area, surface area, and volume.	
Find the area of right triangles, other triangles, special quadrilaterals, and polygons by composing into rectangles or decomposing into triangles and other shapes; apply these techniques in the context of solving real-world and mathematical problems.	85–88
Find the volume of a right rectangular prism with fractional edge lengths by packing it with unit cubes of the appropriate unit fraction edge lengths, and show that the volume is the same as would be found by multiplying the edge lengths of the prism. Apply the formulas $V = l\,w\,h$ and $V = b\,h$ to find volumes of right rectangular prisms with fractional edge lengths in the context of solving real-world and mathematical problems.	89–92
Statistics and Probability	
Summarize and describe distributions.	
Display numerical data in plots on a number line, including dot plots, histograms, and box plots.	93–96, 97–100
Summarize numerical data sets in relation to their context, such as by:	93–100
Reporting the number of observations.	93–96
Giving quantitative measures of center (median and/or mean) and variability (interquartile range and/or mean absolute deviation), as well as describing any overall pattern and any striking deviations from the overall pattern with reference to the context in which the data were gathered.	97–100

Test A Name: ____________________

Directions: Read each problem carefully and select the best answer.

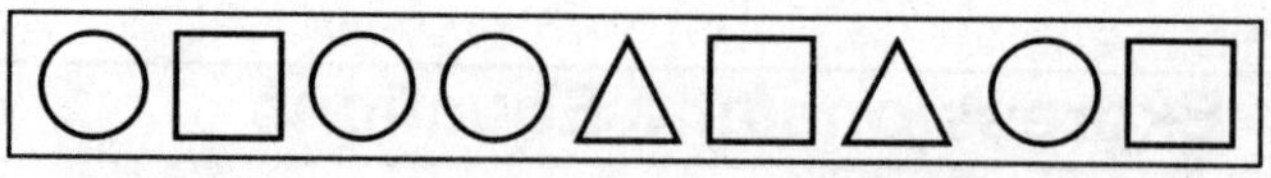

Use the picture to answer questions 1 and 2.

1. Which three ratios show the relationship of the number of triangles to the total number of shapes?

   A. 2:4, $\frac{2}{4}$, 2 to 4

   B. 2:9, $\frac{2}{9}$, 2 to 9

   C. 9:2, $\frac{9}{2}$, 9 to 2

   D. 2:3, $\frac{2}{3}$, 2 to 3

Count the number of shapes and the number of triangles; write the numbers in the correct order.

2. Which three ratios show the relationship of the number of circles to the number of squares?

   A. 4:3, $\frac{4}{3}$, 4 to 3

   B. 3:4, $\frac{3}{4}$, 3 to 4

   C. 4:9, $\frac{4}{9}$, 4 to 9

   D. 4:3, $\frac{4}{3}$, 3 to 4

Think about it! What two shapes are being compared?

3. There are 10 girls and 14 boys in Mrs. Verma's class. What is the ratio of boys to girls?

   A. 10:14

   B. $\frac{10}{14}$

   C. 14:10

   D. 10 to 14

Remember that the order of the numbers in a ratio is important.

4. Naveen planted 3 rows of tomatoes in his garden and 5 rows of watermelon. What is the ratio of rows of tomatoes to rows of watermelon in Naveen's garden? *Hint: More than one answer can be correct.*

   A. 5 to 3

   B. 3:5

   C. 5:3

   D. $\frac{3}{5}$

Pay attention! There is more than one way to correctly write a ratio.

Test A Name: ____________________

Directions: Read each problem carefully and select the best answer.

5. Complete the ratio table.

A. 13
B. 11
C. 21
D. 12

9	3
18	6
27	9
36	
45	15

Look for patterns in the ratio table to help solve the problem.

6. The ratio of the number of days in the week to the number of days Kala goes to school is 7 to 5. Complete the ratio table below to find how many days have passed by the time Kala has gone to school for 15 days.

A. 21
B. 12
C. 17
D. 25

Days Passed	Days at School
7	5
14	10
	15
28	20
35	25

As the numbers in the columns increase, what are they being multiplied by?

7. While watching television, the Deepak family noticed that the movie they were watching was interrupted every 15 minutes for a 2 minute commercial. How many minutes of commercials did they watch in 60 minutes?

A. 6 minutes
B. 7.5 minutes
C. 8 minutes
D. 30 minutes

Total Time Watching	Minutes of Commercials
15	2

The same operation should be used on both terms of the ratio to solve the problem.

8. Kala is making lemonade for the school picnic. For every 2 packets of lemonade powder she must add 4 quarts of water. How much water will she add to 10 packets of lemonade powder?

A. 8 quarts of water
B. 20 quarts of water
C. 9 quarts of water
D. 12 quarts of water

Packets	Quarts of Water
2	4

Remember, both terms of the ratio should be multiplied by 2, 3, 4, etc. until the problem is solved.

Test A **Name:** ______________________

Directions: Read each problem carefully and select the best answer.

9. Find the rate and unit rate given the following information: 600 miles in 12 hours.

A. rate = $\frac{\text{600 miles}}{\text{12 hours}}$; unit rate = $\frac{\text{50 miles}}{\text{1 hour}}$

B. rate = $\frac{\text{12 hours}}{\text{600 miles}}$; unit rate = $\frac{\text{0.02 hour}}{\text{1 mile}}$

C. rate = $\frac{\text{600 miles}}{\text{12 hours}}$; unit rate = $\frac{\text{50 miles}}{\text{12 hours}}$

D. rate = $\frac{\text{12 hours}}{\text{600 miles}}$; unit rate = $\frac{\text{50 miles}}{\text{1 hour}}$

SHOW YOUR WORK!

Think about it! If you know the rate, you can *divide* to find the unit rate.

10. Find the rate and unit rate given the following information: ₹48 for 6 kilograms.

A. rate = $\frac{\text{6 kilograms}}{\text{₹48}}$; unit rate = $\frac{\text{1.125 kilograms}}{\text{₹1}}$

B. rate = $\frac{\text{₹48}}{\text{6 kilograms}}$; unit rate = $\frac{\text{₹8}}{\text{6 kilograms}}$

C. rate = $\frac{\text{6 kilograms}}{\text{₹48}}$; unit rate = $\frac{\text{₹8}}{\text{1 kilograms}}$

D. rate = $\frac{\text{₹48}}{\text{6 kilograms}}$; unit rate = $\frac{\text{₹8}}{\text{1 kilogram}}$

SHOW YOUR WORK!

Remember, in the unit rate, the second number is always 1.

11. Nitin drove 145 kilometres in 5 hours. If he continues to drive at the same rate, how many kilometres will he drive in 8 hours?

A. 148 kilometres

B. 232 kilometres

C. 87 kilometres

D. 145 kilometres

SHOW YOUR WORK!

Pay Attention! How many hours will Nitin drive?

12. Farmer Deepak's prize hen laid 24 eggs in 4 days. If the hen continues to lay eggs at the same rate, how many eggs will she lay in 7 days?

A. 18 eggs

B. 6 eggs

C. 42 eggs

D. 56 eggs

SHOW YOUR WORK!

Find the ratio of eggs to days first.

Test A Name: ____________________

Directions: Read each problem carefully and select the best answer.

13. Change the percent to a fraction to find 4% of 250.

A. 10
B. 100
C. 1,000
D. $62\frac{1}{2}$

SHOW YOUR WORK!

Use what you know! The word *of* means multiply.

14. Change the percent to a fraction to find 48% of 300.

A. 14,400
B. $\frac{1}{144}$
C. 144
D. $14\frac{2}{5}$

SHOW YOUR WORK!

Think about it! Percent means *per 100.*

15. Mike will give the waitress a 15% tip. The bill for his dinner is ₹35.40. How much will the waitress receive for a tip?

A. ₹40.71
B. ₹531
C. ₹5.31
D. ₹53.10

SHOW YOUR WORK!

Reread the problem. Did you answer the question that was asked?

16. The cafeteria staff prepared 60 kilograms of lasagna. From the lasagna prepared, 80% was sold and 20% was donated to the local fire department for lunch. How much lasagna was donated?

A. 48 kilograms
B. 12 kilograms
C. 3 kilograms
D. 30 kilograms

SHOW YOUR WORK!

Remember, a percent can be changed to a fraction to solve the problem.

Test A Name: ____________

Directions: Read each problem carefully and select the best answer. Answers must be in simplest form.

17. Find the quotient.

$\frac{5}{6} \div \frac{6}{10}$

A. $\frac{1}{2}$

B. $\frac{18}{25}$

C. $1\frac{7}{18}$

D. $\frac{25}{18}$

SHOW YOUR WORK!

Cross-cancel (reduce) to make multiplication easier.

18. Find the quotient.

$\frac{4}{7} \div \frac{3}{4}$

A. $\frac{21}{16}$

B. $\frac{3}{7}$

C. $\frac{12}{21}$

D. $\frac{16}{21}$

SHOW YOUR WORK!

Remember to rewrite the division problem as a multiplication problem using the reciprocal of the divisor.

19. Reeta has $\frac{4}{5}$ of a kilogram of cheese. How many $\frac{2}{10}$-kilogram servings does she have?

A. $\frac{4}{25}$ serving

B. 4 servings

C. $\frac{1}{4}$ serving

D. $\frac{4}{1}$ servings

SHOW YOUR WORK!

Divide the $\frac{4}{5}$ kilogram of cheese into $\frac{2}{10}$ kilogram servings. How many servings do you get?

20. Geeta has a piece of material that is $\frac{8}{12}$ metre long. She wants to cut the material into pieces that are $\frac{1}{3}$ metre long. How many $\frac{1}{3}$-metre pieces of material can she make?

A. 2 pieces

B. $\frac{2}{9}$ piece

C. $\frac{8}{4}$ pieces

D. $\frac{1}{2}$ piece

SHOW YOUR WORK!

Take a quick look! Is the answer simplified?

Test A **Name:** ______________________

Directions: Read each problem carefully and select the best answer.

21. Find the quotient.

3,247 ÷ 45

A. 72
B. 74 R17
C. 72 R7
D. 69 R142

SHOW YOUR WORK!

45 is too great to go into 32; start by dividing into 324.

22. Divide.

6,981 ÷ 287

A. 24 R93
B. 24 R193
C. 24 R103
D. 24

SHOW YOUR WORK!

Look at the answer choices to help with the first step of division. All answer choices begin with 2, so 698 ÷ 287 must begin with 2.

23. Find the quotient.

9,390 ÷ 104

A. 93
B. 90 R30
C. 90
D. 9 R30

SHOW YOUR WORK!

Check your answer by multiplying the quotient by the divisor and then add the remainder.

24. A new bookstore needed 7,719 books to complete their inventory. The store received the same number of books every day in the month of May to complete their inventory. How many books did the bookstore receive each day?

A. 257 R3 books
B. 249 days
C. 248 R31 books
D. 249 books

SHOW YOUR WORK!

There are 31 days in the month of May.

Test A Name: ______________________

Directions: Read each problem carefully and select the best answer.

25. Find the sum.

14.57 + 79.668

A. 0.81125
B. 94.238
C. 93.238
D. 9.4238

SHOW YOUR WORK!

Align the decimal points when you add.

26. Find the difference.

51.6 – 28.379

A. 2.3221
B. 23.331
C. 79.979
D. 23.221

SHOW YOUR WORK!

Remember to align the decimals and insert zeros so all numbers have the same amount of digits after the decimal.

27. Find the product.

8.498 × 6.2

A. 52.6876
B. 526.876
C. 52687.6
D. 6.7984

SHOW YOUR WORK!

Count the number of places after the decimals in both factors; in the product, move the decimal one place to the left for each decimal place in the factors.

28. Find the quotient.

197.4 ÷ 1.2

A. 16.45
B. 164
C. 164.5
D. 1.645

SHOW YOUR WORK!

Add zeros after the decimal point in the dividend and divide until there is no remainder.

Test A Name: ____________________

Directions: Read each problem carefully and select the best answer.

29. What is the greatest common factor (GCF) of 12 and 30?

A. 3
B. 2
C. 10
D. 6

SHOW YOUR WORK!

List the factors of each number. Circle the greatest factor that is common to both numbers.

30. What is the greatest common factor (GCF) of 18 and 36?

A. 9
B. 18
C. 6
D. 3

SHOW YOUR WORK!

Did you list all the factors for each number?

31. Which two numbers have a greatest common factor of 8?

A. 4 and 32
B. 18 and 27
C. 16 and 24
D. 35 and 40

SHOW YOUR WORK!

List the factors for each pair of numbers, and circle the GCF for each pair.

32. Which pair of numbers is correctly listed with its GCF?

A. 22 and 44: GCF = 11
B. 21 and 70: GCF = 7
C. 15 and 45: GCF = 5
D. 24 and 36: GCF = 6

SHOW YOUR WORK!

Remember, the GCF is the greatest number that divides evenly into both numbers.

Test A **Name:** ____________________

Directions: Read each problem carefully and select the best answer.

33. What is the least common multiple (LCM) of 4 and 5?

A. 40
B. 15
C. 20
D. 32

SHOW YOUR WORK!

Find *multiples* by multiplying a number by an integer. *Example:* 8 is a multiple of 4 because $4 \times 2 = 8$.

34. What is the least common multiple (LCM) of 8 and 12?

A. 24
B. 96
C. 72
D. 48

SHOW YOUR WORK!

List the multiples of each number. Circle the *least* multiple *common* to both numbers.

35. Which pair of numbers is listed with its LCM?

A. 5 and 10: LCM = 20
B. 3 and 7: LCM = 42
C. 8 and 10: LCM = 40
D. 4 and 9: LCM = 72

SHOW YOUR WORK!

Make sure the LCM is the least number that appears in the lists of multiples for both numbers.

36. Which pair of numbers has an LCM of 9?

A. 3 and 18
B. 3 and 9
C. 9 and 18
D. 3 and 12

SHOW YOUR WORK!

Make a list of multiples for each number; circle the LCM for each pair.

Test A **Name:** ____________________

Directions: Read each problem carefully and select the best answer.

37. Which expression is equal to 24 + 8?

A. 3(8 + 2)
B. 8(3 + 1)
C. (4 × 6) × (4 × 2)
D. (4 × 6) – (4 + 8)

SHOW YOUR WORK!

Find the sum of the given expression, then simplify each answer choice to find which one is equal to that sum.

38. Which expression is equal to 15 + 10?

A. 5(3 × 2)
B. (5 × 5) + (5 × 2)
C. 3(5 + 2)
D. (5 × 3) + (5 × 2)

SHOW YOUR WORK!

Find the greatest common factor of 15 and 10; divide both numbers by the GCF to get started.

39. Which value makes the expression true?

36 + 12 = __ (3 + 1)

A. 12
B. 4
C. 9
D. 3

SHOW YOUR WORK!

Substitute each number in the blank and solve.

40. Which expression is equal to 3(9 + 4)?

A. 12 + 7
B. (3 × 9) + (3 × 4)
C. (3 × 9) × (3 × 4)
D. 27 + 7

SHOW YOUR WORK!

Use the distributive property: multiply both 9 and 4 by 3.

Test A **Name:** ____________________

Directions: Read each problem carefully and select the best answer.

For six days in a row, Sudhakar played his favourite game online. Below is a summary of points for each day that he played.

DAY	POINT SUMMARY
1	gained 20 points
2	gained 25 points
3	lost 25 points
4	lost 20 points
5	lost 35 points
6	gained 35 points

41. Which integer represents the points Sudhakar earned on day 2?

A. -25
B. 35
C. 25
D. -20

Sudhakar gained points on day two, so the integer is positive.

42. On which day was Sudhakar's score -20?

A. day 1
B. day 2
C. day 3
D. day 4

When you lose points, it is a negative number.

43. Which integer shows Sudhakar's lowest score?

A. -35
B. -20
C. 20
D. -25

The further away the negative number is from zero, the lower the score.

44. Which integer is the opposite of 25?

A. 25
B. -25
C. -35
D. 50

Negative numbers and positive numbers are exact opposites.

Test A **Name:** ____________________

Directions: Read each problem carefully and select the best answer.

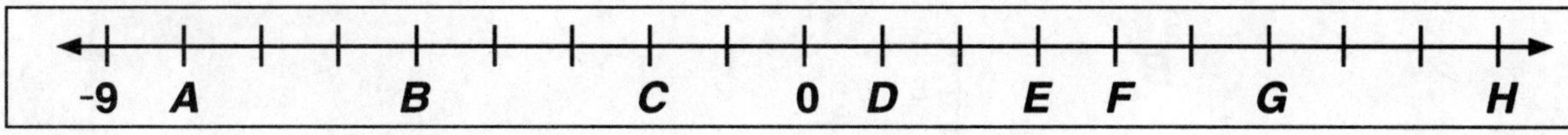

Use the number line to answer questions 45 and 46.

45. Which point on the number line is the opposite of -3?

A. *B*
B. *E*
C. *D*
D. *F*

> The opposite of a negative number is a positive number.

46. Which point of the number line is the opposite of 8?

A. *H*
B. *G*
C. *C*
D. *A*

> The opposite of a positive number is a negative number.

47. Which integer equals -(-4)?

A. -4
B. -(4)
C. 4
D. -(-5)

> The opposite of the opposite of a number is the number itself.

48. Which integer is the opposite of 10?

A. -10
B. $\frac{10}{1}$
C. $\frac{1}{10}$
D. none of the above

> Opposite numbers are equidistant from 0 on the number line but in opposite directions.

Test A Name: ________________

Directions: Read each problem carefully and select the best answer.

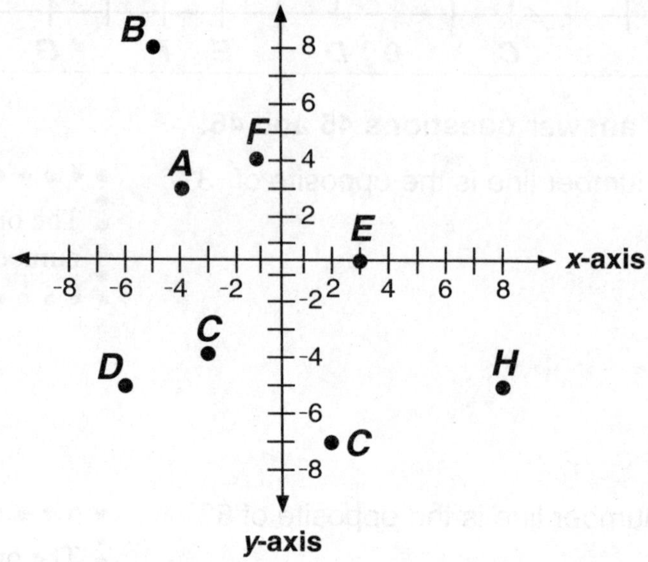

49. Which point is located at (-3,-4)?

A. *C* **C.** *A*

B. *F* **D.** *G*

> Starting from the origin (0,0), first move left or right; then move up or down.

50. Which point is located at (-5,8)?

A. *H* **C.** *B*

B. *D* **D.** *E*

> A negative *x* value is to the left of the origin; a positive *y* value is above the origin.

51. Which ordered pair is located at point *F*?

A. (-1,4) **C.** (3,0)

B. (2,-7) **D.** (-6,-6)

> The first coordinate tells how far to move on the *x*-axis; the second coordinate tells how far to move on the *y*-axis.

52. Which ordered pair is located at point *A*?

A. (8,-5) **C.** (-3,-4)

B. (-4,3) **D.** (-5,8)

> Which coordinate(s) should be positive? Which coordinate(s) should be negative?

Test A Name: ____________________

Directions: Read each problem carefully and select the best answer.

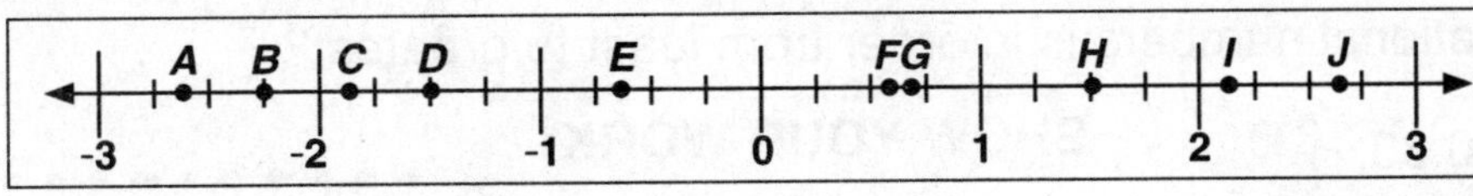

53. Which point is located at -1.91?

A. *J*
B. *C*
C. *A*
D. *F*

SHOW YOUR WORK!

-1.91 is to the left of zero and is located between -1 and -2. Think: Is 1.91 closer to 1 or to 2?

54. Which point is located at 1.5?

A. *D*
B. *I*
C. *H*
D. *F*

SHOW YOUR WORK!

Think about which two integers 1.5 is between.

55. Which rational number is located at point *A*?

A. 2.6
B. $\frac{17}{8}$
C. $-\frac{9}{4}$
D. -2.6

SHOW YOUR WORK!

Change improper fractions to decimals to see which integers they are between.

56. Which rational number is located at point *G*?

A. $-\frac{9}{4}$
B. 0.67
C. $\frac{3}{5}$
D. -0.7

SHOW YOUR WORK!

Is *G* negative or positive?

Test A Name: ____________________

Directions: Read each problem carefully and select the best answer.

57. Which set of rational numbers is in order from least to greatest?

A. $-1.4, -\frac{12}{5}, -0.33, -\frac{2}{3}$

B. $-0.33, -\frac{2}{3}, -1.4, -\frac{12}{5}$

C. $-\frac{12}{5}, -1.4, -0.33, -\frac{2}{3}$

D. $-\frac{12}{5}, -1.4, -\frac{2}{3}, -0.33$

SHOW YOUR WORK!

Change all the numbers to the same format—decimals—to compare.

58. Which set of rational numbers is in order from greatest to least?

A. $-4\frac{1}{8}, -3.12, 1.15, \frac{11}{8}$

B. $\frac{11}{8}, 1.15, -3.12, -4\frac{1}{8}$

C. $1.15, \frac{11}{8}, -3.12, -4\frac{1}{8}$

D. $\frac{11}{8}, 1.15, -4\frac{1}{8}, -3.12$

SHOW YOUR WORK!

The further away from zero on the left, the less the value of the rational number.

59. Which set of rational numbers is in order from greatest to least?

A. $1\frac{3}{4}, \frac{5}{8}, 0.4, -5\frac{3}{7}$

B. $-5\frac{3}{7}, 1\frac{3}{4}, \frac{5}{8}, 0.4$

C. $1\frac{3}{4}, \frac{5}{8}, -5\frac{3}{7}, 0.4$

D. $0.4, \frac{5}{8}, 1\frac{3}{4}, -5\frac{3}{7}$

SHOW YOUR WORK!

Eliminate answer choices where the negative number is not last. Since there is only one negative number, it is the least.

60. Which set of rational numbers is in order from least to greatest?

A. $-3\frac{3}{4}, \frac{7}{2}, -3.62, 3.81$

B. $3.81, \frac{7}{2}, -3.62, -3\frac{3}{4}$

C. $-3\frac{3}{4}, -3.62, \frac{7}{2}, 3.81$

D. $-3.62, -3\frac{3}{4}, \frac{7}{2}, 3.81$

SHOW YOUR WORK!

Convert $-3\frac{3}{4}$ to a decimal to find if it is less than -3.62 or greater than -3.62.

Test A Name: ____________________

Directions: Read each problem carefully and select the best answer.

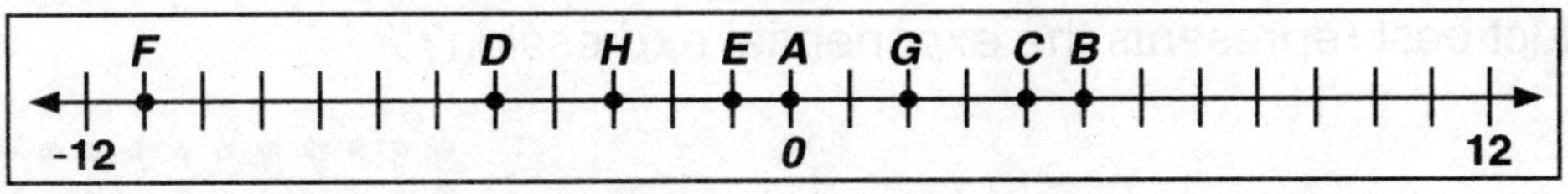

Use the number line to answer questions 61 and 62.

61. Which set of numbers shows the integer naming point *B* on the number line followed by its absolute value?

A. 5 and 5
B. 5 and -5
C. -5 and 5
D. -5 and -5

> The absolute value of an integer is its distance from zero; can distance be negative?

62. Which set of numbers shows the integer naming point *H* on the number line followed by its absolute value?

A. 3 and 3
B. -3 and -3
C. -3 and 3
D. 3 and -3

> Pay attention to the sign of the integer.

63. Death Valley California is 282 feet below sea level. Which set of numbers shows the integer representing Death Valley's elevation followed by the absolute value of the integer?

A. -282 and -282
B. 282 and 282
C. 282 and -282
D. -282 and 282

> Think about what *below* sea level means.

64. Over the last three days, Pierceburg had the coldest temperatures ever recorded in the area. On Friday and Saturday it was -12°, and on Sunday it was -7°. Which day(s) of the weekend was the warmest?

A. Friday
B. Saturday
C. Sunday
D. Friday and Saturday

> Use what you know! Think about a thermometer to decide which temperature is warmer.

Test A Name: ____________________

Directions: Read each problem carefully and select the best answer.

65. Which product best represents the exponential expression?

8^4

A. $4 \times 4 \times 4 \times 4 \times 4 \times 4 \times 4 \times 4$
B. $8 \times 8 \times 8 \times 8$
C. 8×4
D. none of the above

Remember that exponential expressions are a convenient way to write repeated multiplication of a number by itself.

66. Evaluate the exponential expression.

8^4

A. 32
B. 12
C. 2
D. 4,096

SHOW YOUR WORK!

The *base* number is the factor that is being multiplied.

67. Expand the exponential expression.

6^3

A. 6×3
B. $6 \times 6 \times 6$
C. $3 \times 3 \times 3 \times 3 \times 3 \times 3$
D. none of the above

The *exponent* tells how many times the base number is used as a factor.

68. Evaluate the exponential expression.

6^3

A. 729
B. 2
C. 216
D. 18

SHOW YOUR WORK!

Expand the exponential expression into a multiplication sentence to evaluate.

Test A Name: ______________

Directions: Read each problem carefully and select the algebraic expression that best represents the given word expression.

69. the product of 3 and a number n

A. $n + 3$
B. $n - 3$
C. $3n$
D. $n \div 3$

The phrases *the product of* and *times* indicate multiplication.

70. 8 less than a number b

A. $b - 8$
B. $8 + b$
C. $8 - b$
D. $8 \div b$

Order matters. Your expression should start with b then be reduced by 8.

71. 36 divided by a number f

A. $f \div 36$
B. $36f$
C. $36 + f$
D. $36 \div f$

Pay attention! Order matters.

72. 2 less than 5 times a number t

A. $2 - 5t$
B. $5t - 2$
C. $3 \times t$
D. $(5 - 2) \times t$

Be careful! First decide on the operations, then decide how to write the expression.

Test A Name: ____________

Directions: Read each problem carefully and select the best answer.

73. Evaluate the expression for $b = 6$.

$b^2 - 4(4) + b \div 2$

A. –1
B. 67
C. 23
D. none of the above

SHOW YOUR WORK!

The variable must be replaced with the value given.

74. Evaluate the expression for $x = 5$.

$x^3 - 5(5) + 2x$

A. 110
B. 0
C. 3,010
D. none of the above

SHOW YOUR WORK!

Follow the order of operations.

75. At Bowl-O-Rama, bowling costs ₹3.00 per game and shoe rental is ₹1.00. Use the expression $3g + 1$ to determine how much it will cost Amit to rent shoes and bowl 2 games.

A. ₹8
B. ₹4
C. ₹5
D. ₹7

SHOW YOUR WORK!

Pay attention to which number should be substituted into the expression.

76. Ferheena charges ₹9 per hour for babysitting and an additional ₹5 if she needs to prepare a meal. On Saturday she babysat for 6 hours and prepared lunch. Use the expression $9h + 5$ to determine how much Ferheena charged her neighbor for babysitting on Saturday.

A. ₹14
B. ₹59
C. ₹84
D. ₹54

SHOW YOUR WORK!

Be sure to replace *h* with the correct value.

Test A **Name:** ______________________

Directions: Use the distributive property to find an equivalent expression.

77. $7(x + 9)$

A. $x + 63$
B. $7x + 63$
C. $7x + 16$
D. $7x + 9$

SHOW YOUR WORK!

Remember that the distributive property involves multiplying.

78. $36x + 18y$

A. $18(2x + y)$
B. $54xy$
C. $2(36x + 18y)$
D. $18(2x + 18y)$

SHOW YOUR WORK!

Begin by finding the GCF of 36 and 18; the GCF goes outside of the parentheses.

79. $5(y - 5)$

A. $y - 25$
B. $5y - 5$
C. $5y - 25$
D. none of the above

SHOW YOUR WORK!

Multiply each term inside the parentheses by the number outside.

80. $24 + 48y$

A. $72y$
B. $24(1 + 2y)$
C. $12(2y + 4y)$
D. $24(24 + 2y)$

SHOW YOUR WORK!

Check your answer by multiplying the terms inside the parentheses by the term outside the parentheses. It should equal the original expression.

Test A Name: ______________________

Directions: Read each problem carefully and select the best answer.

81. Which value, when substituted for x, makes the equation true?

$9 + 3x = 21$

A. 7
B. 12
C. 9
D. 4

SHOW YOUR WORK!

Substitute means to replace the variable with the given number.

82. Which value, when substituted for y, makes the inequality true?

$32 - y > 14 + 7$

A. 12
B. 8
C. 11
D. 21

SHOW YOUR WORK!

Replace y with each answer choice, and simplify both sides of the inequality to see which value makes it true.

83. Which equation is true when $n = 6$?

A. $4 + 2n = 12$
B. $3 \times (3n) = 36$
C. $54 \div n = 9$
D. $19 - n + 3 = 13$

SHOW YOUR WORK!

Replace n in each equation with 6 and follow the order of operations to solve.

84. Which open sentence is true when $n = 5$?

A. $3 + n < 8$
B. $25 - n = 30$
C. $7 \times n = 35$
D. $40 \div (2n) = 8$

SHOW YOUR WORK!

Look carefully at each symbol. Solve by substituting 5 in place of the n.

Test A Name: ____________

Directions: Read each problem carefully and select the best answer.

85. Find the area of the parallelogram.

A. 48 in.^{2}
B. 24 in.
C. 48 in.
D. 24 in.^{2}

SHOW YOUR WORK!

A rectangle is a parallelogram.

86. Find the area of the triangle.

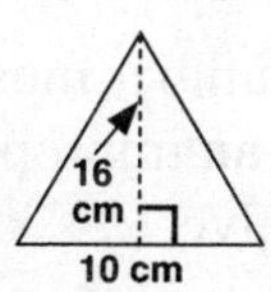

A. 80 cm
B. 160 cm^2
C. 160 cm
D. 80 cm^2

SHOW YOUR WORK!

Area is always measured in square units.

87. Find the area of the triangle.

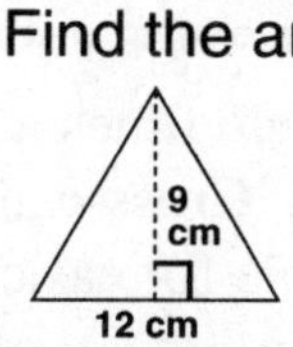

A. 108 cm^2
B. 54 cm
C. 54 cm^2
D. 108 cm

SHOW YOUR WORK!

Look at the triangle. The dotted line in the middle indicates the height.

88. Find the area of the trapezoid.

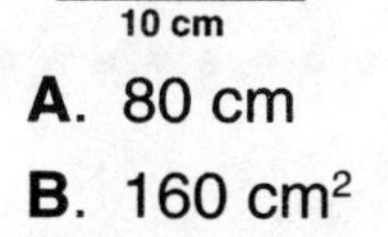

A. 88 in.
B. 11 in.^{2}
C. 11 in.
D. 88 in.^{2}

SHOW YOUR WORK!

The parallel sides of the trapezoid are called base$_1$ and base$_2$.

Test A Name: ________________

Directions: Read each problem carefully and select the best answer.

89. Find the volume of the rectangular prism.

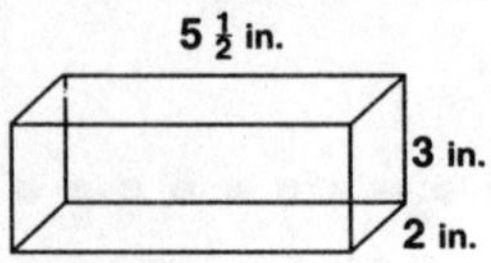

A. 33 in.^{2}
B. 33 in.^{3}
C. 66 in.^{3}
D. $10\frac{1}{2}$ in.^{3}

SHOW YOUR WORK!

Volume is measured in cubic units (unit^3).

90. Find the volume of the rectangular prism.

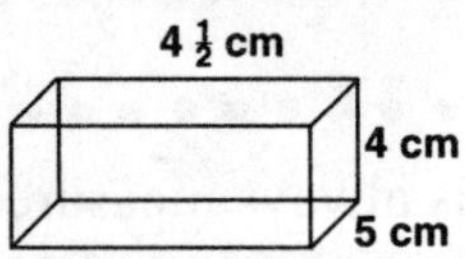

A. 90 cm^3
B. 180 cm^3
C. $13\frac{1}{2}$ cm^3
D. 90 cm^2

SHOW YOUR WORK!

The mixed number must be converted to an improper fraction to solve.

91. Find the volume of the rectangular prism.

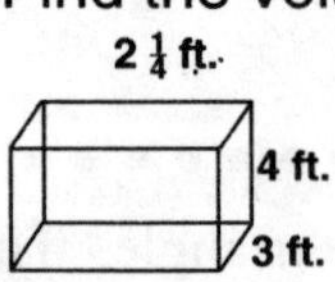

A. $9\frac{1}{4}$ ft.^{2}
B. 27 ft.^{2}
C. 108 ft.^{3}
D. 27 ft.^{3}

SHOW YOUR WORK!

Multiply *length* times *width* times *height*. Cross-cancel where possible for easier multiplication.

92. Find the volume of the rectangular prism.

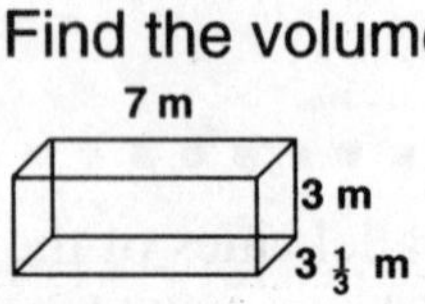

A. 70 m^2
B. 210 m^3
C. $13\frac{1}{3}$ m^3
D. 70 m^3

SHOW YOUR WORK!

Use multiplication to find volume.

Test A Name: ____________________

Directions: Read each problem carefully and select the best answer.

A meteorologist kept track of the number of rainy days in 2013. The results were recorded on the dot plot below.

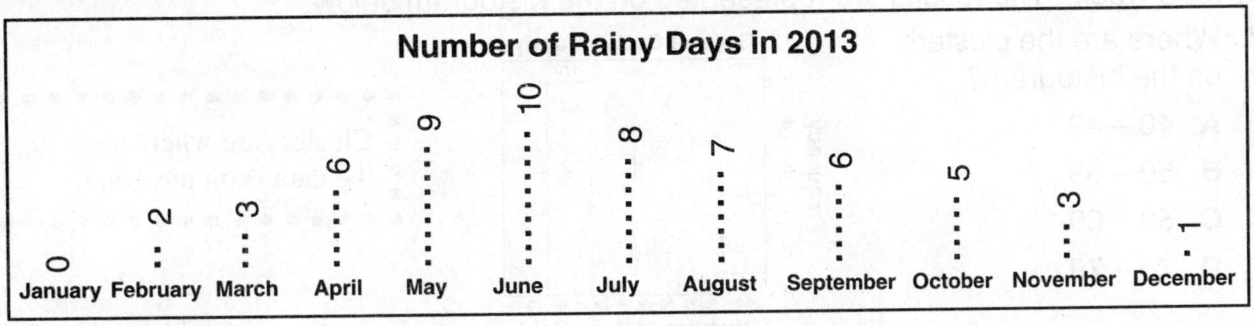

93. What is the total number of rainy days observed in 2013?

A. 54 days
B. 60 days
C. 55 days
D. 51 days

SHOW YOUR WORK!

Add all the data to find the total number of rainy days observed.

94. What is the mean number of rainy days in 2013?

A. 12 days
B. 10 days
C. 5 days
D. 5.5 days

SHOW YOUR WORK!

The *mean* is the average. Add all the data values together and divide by the number of values added (12).

95. What is the median of the data?

A. 5.5 days
B. 5 days
C. 6 days
D. 0 days

SHOW YOUR WORK!

Find the *median* of an even number of values by listing the data in order from least to greatest. Add the two numbers in the middle, and then divide by two.

96. Identify the outlier in the dot plot.

A. 0
B. 10
C. 1
D. There is no outlier.

Outliers are data points that lie far away from other data points.

Test A Name: ____________________

Directions: Read each problem carefully and select the best answer.

The vendor at the amusement park recorded the amount of cotton candy sold each day for a week. The results are represented on the histogram below.

97. Where are the clusters on the histogram?

A. 40 – 49
B. 50 – 59
C. 50 – 69
D. 70 – 79

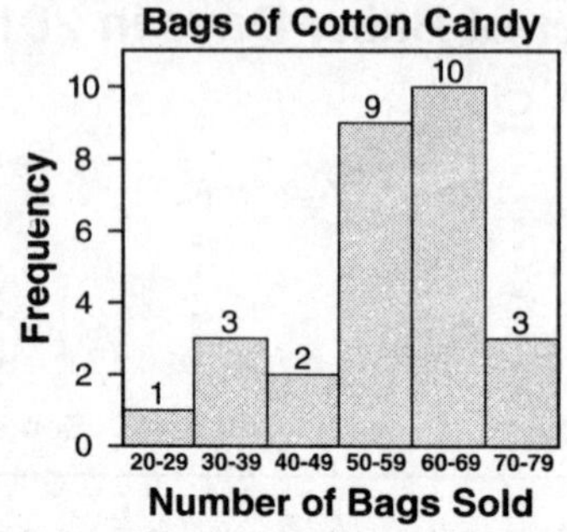

Clusters are where most of the data is on the graph.

Use the box plot and the list of values to answer questions 98–100.

8, 4, 10, 4, 5, 10, 8

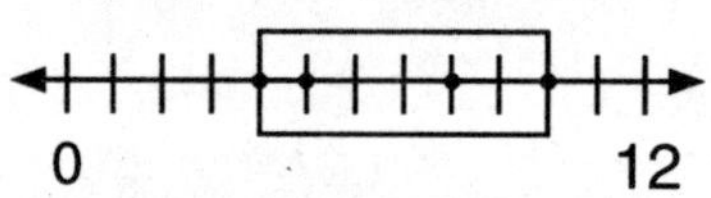

98. What is the median value of the data?

A. 8
B. 10
C. 5
D. 4

SHOW YOUR WORK!

The *median* is the middle number in the data, or the value in the middle of the box.

99. What is the mean absolute deviation?

A. 49
B. 16
C. 7
D. 2.28

SHOW YOUR WORK!

Calculate the mean absolute deviation by finding the mean first: add all the values and divide by 7 (the number of values). Then find the difference between the mean and each value in the list. Add the differences and divide by 7 (the number of values).

100. What is the interquartile range?

A. 10
B. 6
C. 4
D. 49

SHOW YOUR WORK!

Subtract the 1st quartile from the 3rd quartile to calculate the interquartile range.

Test B Name: ____________________

Directions: Read each problem carefully and select the best answer.

○ △ ○ ○ □ △ □ ○ □ ○

Use the picture to answer questions 1–2.

1. Which three ratios show the relationship of the number of triangles to the number of squares?

SHOW YOUR WORK!

A. 3:2, $\frac{3}{2}$, 3 to 2

B. 2:5, $\frac{2}{5}$, 2 to 5

C. 2:10, $\frac{2}{10}$, 2 to 10

D. 2:3, $\frac{2}{3}$, 2 to 3

Are the numbers in the correct order?

2. Which three ratios show the relationship of the number of circles to the number of squares?

SHOW YOUR WORK!

A. 3:5, $\frac{3}{5}$, 3 to 5

B. 5:2, $\frac{5}{2}$, 5 to 2

C. 5:3, $\frac{5}{3}$, 5 to 3

D. 5:10, $\frac{5}{10}$, 5 to 10

3. Bharti Middle School held an election for class president. 221 students voted in all. Naveen received 123 votes and Deepak received 98 votes. What is the ratio of votes Deepak received to the number of votes Naveen received?

A. 123:98

B. 98:123

C. 221:98

D. 123:221

Be sure to use the correct numbers; extra information is given in this problem.

4. Ferheena and Seeta baked cookies for their class party. They baked 12 peanut butter cookies, 24 chocolate chip cookies, and 6 oatmeal raisin cookies. What is the ratio of peanut butter cookies to the total number of cookies baked?

SHOW YOUR WORK!

A. 42:12

B. 12:30

C. 12:42

D. 30:12

Test B **Name:** ____________________

Directions: Read each problem carefully and select the best answer.

5. Complete the ratio table.

A. 21
B. 19
C. 20
D. 17

2	5
4	10
6	15
8	
10	25

Figure out the relationship between 2 and 4 and between 5 and 10. Continue the pattern down the column.

6. For every ₹6 Sunita earns by selling raffle tickets for her school, ₹4 is deposited into her personal account to help pay for her field trip to Simla. If Sunita has sold ₹18 worth of raffle tickets so far, how much money has been deposited into her personal account?

A. ₹14
B. ₹12
C. ₹11
D. ₹13

Money Collected	Money Deposited to Personal Account
₹6	₹4
₹12	₹8
₹18	
₹24	₹16
₹30	₹20

7. Naveen wanted to know how many gallons of petrol he would need to drive to his friend's cabin 160 miles north of his own home. He knew that it took 2 gallons of petrol to drive 32 miles. At this same rate, how many gallons of petrol would he need to drive to his friend's cabin? Use the ratio table to help you solve the problem.

A. 6 gallons
B. 7 gallons
C. 160 gallons
D. 10 gallons

Miles	Gallons

Be sure to place the values in the correct columns in the table.

8. Seeta plays basketball for her school. She practices 4 days a week. Today her team is practicing free throws, which she is very good at. She shot 10 times and made 7 baskets. If she continues to make free throws at this rate during practice, how many times will she need to shoot to make 35 baskets? Use the ratio table to help you solve the problem.

A. 14 times
B. 50 times
C. 38 times
D. 5 times

Number of Shots Taken	Number of Baskets Made

Test B Name: ____________

Directions: Read each problem carefully and select the best answer.

9. Find the rate and unit rate given the following information: 270 miles on 15 gallons of petrol.

A. rate = $\frac{270 \text{ miles}}{15 \text{ gallons}}$; unit rate = $\frac{18 \text{ miles}}{1 \text{ gallon}}$

B. rate = $\frac{270 \text{ miles}}{15 \text{ gallons}}$; unit rate = $\frac{18 \text{ miles}}{15 \text{ gallons}}$

C. rate = $\frac{15 \text{ gallons}}{270 \text{ miles}}$; unit rate = $\frac{18 \text{ miles}}{1 \text{ gallon}}$

D. none of the above

SHOW YOUR WORK!

Use what you know! The second number in a unit rate is always 1.

10. Find the rate and unit rate given the following information: ₹255 for 5 weeks.

A. rate = $\frac{₹255}{5 \text{ weeks}}$; unit rate = $\frac{₹50}{1 \text{ week}}$

B. rate = $\frac{₹255}{5 \text{ weeks}}$; unit rate = $\frac{₹51}{5 \text{ weeks}}$

C. rate = $\frac{₹255}{5 \text{ weeks}}$; unit rate = $\frac{₹51}{1 \text{ week}}$

D. none of the above

SHOW YOUR WORK!

Remember to the find the rate (ratio) before trying to find the unit rate.

11. It took Vicky 36 minutes to read 9 pages in her new book. If she continues to read at the same rate, how long will it take her to read 27 pages?

A. 972 minutes
B. 108 minutes
C. 4 minutes
D. 81 minutes

SHOW YOUR WORK!

12. There are 144 number-two pencils in 12 boxes. How many pencils would be in 16 boxes?

A. 9 pencils
B. 12 pencils
C. 192 pencils
D. 576 pencils

SHOW YOUR WORK!

Test B Name: ____________________

Directions: Read each problem carefully and select the best answer.

13. Change the percent to a fraction to find 35% of 900.

A. $\frac{1}{315}$
B. $31\frac{1}{2}$
C. 3,150
D. 315

SHOW YOUR WORK!

Remember, *of* is a clue to multiply.

14. Change the percent to a fraction to find 110% of 500.

A. 550
B. 5,500
C. 55
D. $\frac{1}{550}$

SHOW YOUR WORK!

15. A vote for the Best Artist of the Year was held last week. Ferheena received 65% of the votes. A total of 80 people voted. How many votes did Ferheena receive?

A. 48 votes
B. 52 votes
C. 50 votes
D. 15 votes

SHOW YOUR WORK!

16. Ferheena receives a monthly allowance of ₹200. She plans to use 15% of her allowance to purchase a new scrapbook. How much will the scrapbook cost?

A. ₹3
B. ₹300
C. ₹30
D. ₹12

SHOW YOUR WORK!

Is your answer reasonable?

Test B Name: ________________

Directions: Read each problem carefully and select the best answer. Answers must be in simplest form.

17. Find the quotient.

$\frac{9}{10} \div \frac{3}{5}$

A. $\frac{3}{2}$

B. $1\frac{1}{2}$

C. $\frac{2}{3}$

D. $\frac{27}{50}$

SHOW YOUR WORK!

Remember to simplify all answers.

18. Find the quotient.

$\frac{5}{6} \div \frac{3}{8}$

A. $\frac{9}{20}$

B. $\frac{20}{9}$

C. $2\frac{2}{9}$

D. $\frac{5}{16}$

SHOW YOUR WORK!

19. Vicky has $\frac{5}{8}$ gallon of lemonade. How many $\frac{2}{16}$-gallon servings can she pour?

A. $\frac{2}{10}$ serving

B. $\frac{5}{64}$ serving

C. $12\frac{4}{5}$ servings

D. 5 servings

SHOW YOUR WORK!

Reread the question! Which fraction should be the divisor (second number in the division expression)?

20. Nitin is building a new door for his tree house. It is $\frac{7}{8}$ of a metre wide and is made of boards that are $\frac{1}{4}$ metre wide. How many boards will he use to build the door?

A. $\frac{7}{2}$ boards

B. $\frac{2}{7}$ board

C. $3\frac{1}{2}$ boards

D. $4\frac{4}{7}$ boards

SHOW YOUR WORK!

Test B Name: ____________

Directions: Read each problem carefully and select the best answer.

21. Simplify.

5,102 ÷ 83

A. 61 R39
B. 61 R45
C. 51 R39
D. 61

SHOW YOUR WORK!

The divisor (83) is greater than 5 and greater than 51, so begin by dividing the first *three* digits of the dividend by 83.

22. Find the quotient.

3,111 ÷ 29

A. 17 R8
B. 107
C. 106 R37
D. 107 R8

SHOW YOUR WORK!

The remainder cannot be greater than the divisor.

23. Divide.

8,593 ÷ 216

A. 39 R69
B. 39 R169
C. 39
D. 169 R39

SHOW YOUR WORK!

24. The football stadium has 8,198 seats. There are 264 seats in each row. How many rows of seats are in the football stadium?

A. 31 rows R14 rows
B. 31 rows R14 seats
C. 31 rows
D. 31 seats R14 rows

SHOW YOUR WORK!

Test B Name: ____________

Directions: Read each problem carefully and select the best answer.

25. Find the product.

4.77 × 5.4

A. 25.758
B. 2575.8
C. 257.58
D. 25,758

SHOW YOUR WORK!

Count the total number of digits after the decimals in both factors; place the decimal that many places from the right in the product.

26. Find the sum.

37.162 + 9.3

A. 37.255
B. 46.462
C. 4.6462
D. 13.0162

SHOW YOUR WORK!

27. Find the quotient.

0.6 ÷ 0.75

A. 0.9375
B. 0.8
C. 0.008
D. 0.08

SHOW YOUR WORK!

Count the number of places after the decimal point in the divisor. Move the decimal point that number of places to the right in the dividend. Do you need to add zeros?

28. Find the difference.

15.07 – 4.294

A. 10.776
B. 27.87
C. 19.364
D. 1.0776

SHOW YOUR WORK!

Test B Name: ____________________

Directions: Read each problem carefully and select the best answer.

29. What is the greatest common factor (GCF) of 18 and 63?

A. 9
B. 6
C. 3
D. 7

SHOW YOUR WORK!

List the factors of each number. Then circle the greatest factor that is common to both numbers.

30. What is the greatest common factor (GCF) of 24 and 42?

A. 3
B. 4
C. 6
D. 2

SHOW YOUR WORK!

31. Which two numbers have a GCF of 9?

A. 35 and 56
B. 6 and 48
C. 10 and 25
D. 45 and 72

SHOW YOUR WORK!

For which pair of numbers is 9 the greatest number that divides evenly into both of them?

32. Which pair of numbers is correctly listed with its GCF?

A. 14 and 28: GCF = 7
B. 20 and 40: GCF = 10
C. 16 and 20: GCF = 4
D. 45 and 54: GCF = 3

SHOW YOUR WORK!

Test B **Name:** ____________________

Directions: Read each problem carefully and select the best answer.

33. What is the least common multiple (LCM) of 2 and 6?

A. 18
B. 12
C. 30
D. 6

SHOW YOUR WORK!

Remember that a number is also a multiple of itself.

34. What is the least common multiple (LCM) of 3 and 10?

A. 50
B. 30
C. 60
D. 20

SHOW YOUR WORK!

35. Which pair of numbers is correctly listed with its LCM?

A. 7 and 9: LCM = 56
B. 3 and 8: LCM = 48
C. 4 and 12: LCM = 12
D. 5 and 6: LCM = 60

SHOW YOUR WORK!

List the multiples of each number, and circle the *least common* multiple for each pair.

36. Which pair of numbers has an LCM of 6?

A. 3 and 6
B. 3 and 9
C. 12 and 18
D. 6 and 12

SHOW YOUR WORK!

Test B Name: ______

Directions: Read each problem carefully and select the best answer.

37. Which expression is equal to 54 + 18?

A. 6(9 + 2)
B. (9 × 6) × (9 × 2)
C. 9(6 × 2)
D. 9(6 + 2)

SHOW YOUR WORK!

Simplify each answer choice and choose the expression that is equal to 54 + 18.

38. Which expression is equal to 42 + 21?

A. 7(6 + 3)
B. (6 × 7) + (6 × 3)
C. 7(6 × 3)
D. (7 × 6) × (7 × 3)

SHOW YOUR WORK!

Look carefully at the operation signs (+, –, ×, ÷). Simplify each expression.

39. Which number makes the equation true?

28 + 16 = 4 (7 + __)

A. 4
B. 8
C. 2
D. 12

SHOW YOUR WORK!

40. Which expression is equal to 5(8 + 7)?

A. 40 × 35
B. 40 + 35
C. (5 × 8) – (5 × 7)
D. (5 + 8) × (5 + 7)

SHOW YOUR WORK!

Test B Name: ____________________

Directions: Read each problem carefully and select the best answer.

In 2013, Sunil, the weatherman for Memorial High School, recorded the highest and lowest temperatures for five states. The results are shown in the table below.

State	Highest Temperature (relative to zero)	Lowest Temperature (relative to zero)
California	117° above	25° below
Montana	134° above	45° below
Texas	122° above	34° below
New York	101° above	15° below
Delaware	112° above	9° below

41. Which two integers show the high and low temperatures for Texas?

A. high = -122; low = 34
B. high = 122; low = -34
C. high = 122; low = 34
D. high = -122; low = -34

The *above* temperatures are positive integers; the *below* temperatures are negative integers.

42. Which state had the lowest temperature?

A. Delaware
B. New York
C. Montana
D. California

SHOW YOUR WORK!

Look carefully at the integers in the *Lowest Temperature* column. The further away the negative number is from zero, the lower the temperature.

43. Which integer is the opposite of Delaware's highest temperature?

A. 9
B. 112
C. -112
D. -134

44. Which two integers show the high and low temperatures for New York?

A. high = 101; low = -15
B. high = 101; low = 15
C. high = -15; low = 101
D. high = -101; low = -15

Test B Name: ____________________

Directions: Read each problem carefully and select the best answer.

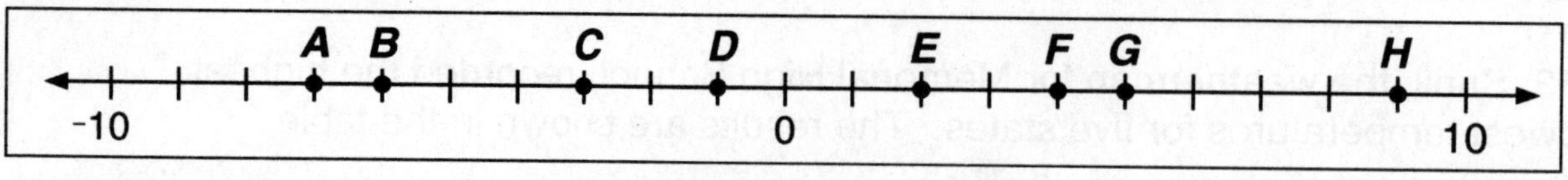

Use the number line to answer questions 45 and 46.

45. Which point on the number line is the opposite of 6?

A. *G*
B. *C*
C. *B*
D. *A*

46. Which point on the number line is the opposite of -9?

A. *H*
B. *G*
C. *E*
D. *D*

> Remember, the opposite of a negative number is a positive number.

47. Which integer is equal to 7?

A. -(7)
B. -7
C. 0
D. -(-7)

48. Which integer is equal to -(-2)?

A. -2
B. 2
C. -(2)
D. 4

> Two negative signs in a row equal a positive.

Test B Name: ____________________

Directions: Read each problem carefully and select the best answer.

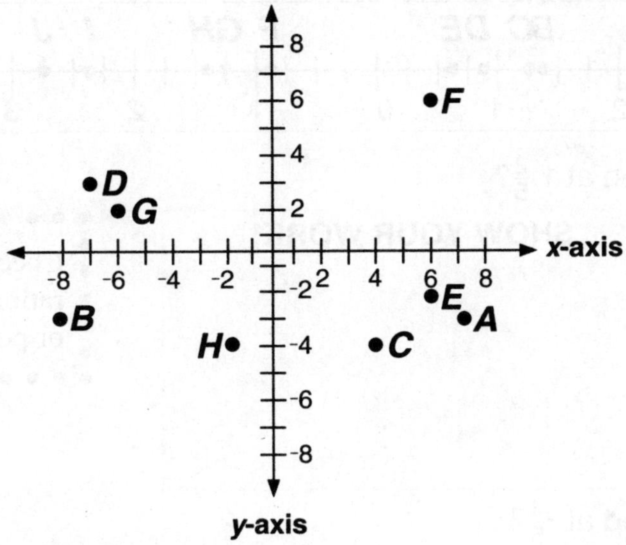

49. Which point is located at (-7,3)?

A. *A** **C.** *B*

B. *D* **D.** *F*

The first number of the ordered pair tells where to move on the *x*-axis.

50. Which point is located at (6,-2)?

A. *G* **C.** *C*

B. *E* **D.** *H*

Pay careful attention to the positive and negative numbers in the ordered pair.

51. Which ordered pair is located at point *H*?

A. (-8,-3) **C.** (4,-4)

B. (1,4) **D.** (-2,-4)

52. Which ordered pair is located at point *C*?

A. (4,-4) **C.** (4,4)

B. (-4,4) **D.** (-4,-4)

Test B Name: ____________________

Directions: Read each problem carefully and select the best answer.

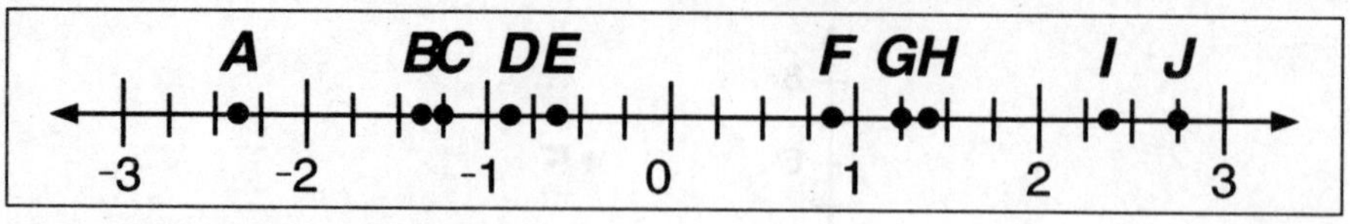

53. Which point is located at $1\frac{2}{5}$?

A. *G*
B. *B*
C. *C*
D. *H*

SHOW YOUR WORK!

Check carefully to see if the rational number is negative or positive.

54. Which point is located at $-\frac{4}{5}$?

A. *F*
B. *J*
C. *E*
D. *D*

SHOW YOUR WORK!

55. Which rational number is located at point *B*?

A. $-1\frac{2}{5}$
B. 2.3
C. $1\frac{1}{4}$
D. $-2\frac{1}{3}$

SHOW YOUR WORK!

Is Point *B* on the left (negative) or the right (positive) of the zero?

56. Which rational number is located at point *J*?

A. $\frac{4}{5}$
B. $\frac{11}{4}$
C. $-\frac{4}{5}$
D. 2.5

SHOW YOUR WORK!

Test B Name: ____________________

Directions: Read each problem carefully and select the best answer.

57. Which set of rational numbers is in order from greatest to least?

A. $-0.8, -\frac{7}{8}, -\frac{10}{7}, -1\frac{5}{6}$

B. $-\frac{7}{8}, -0.8, -\frac{10}{7}, -1\frac{5}{6}$

C. $-0.8, -\frac{7}{8}, -1\frac{5}{6}, -\frac{10}{7}$

D. $-1\frac{5}{6}, -\frac{10}{7}, -\frac{7}{8}, -0.8$

SHOW YOUR WORK!

Change all the rational numbers to decimals.

58. Which set of rational numbers is in order from greatest to least?

A. $2.35, -2.35, -\frac{11}{6}, \frac{3}{5}$

B. $-2.35, -\frac{11}{6}, \frac{3}{5}, 2.35$

C. $2.35, \frac{3}{5}, -\frac{11}{6}, -2.35$

D. $-2.35, \frac{3}{5}, -\frac{11}{6}, 2.35$

SHOW YOUR WORK!

Eliminate answers where the first number listed is negative. Negative numbers are never greater than positive numbers.

59. Which set of rational numbers is in order from least to greatest?

A. $2\frac{2}{3}, \frac{9}{10}, 0.13, -5.1$

B. $-5.1, \frac{9}{10}, 0.13, 2\frac{2}{3}$

C. $2\frac{2}{3}, 0.13, \frac{9}{10}, -5.1$

D. $-5.1, 0.13, \frac{9}{10}, 2\frac{2}{3}$

SHOW YOUR WORK!

60. Which set of rational numbers is in order from least to greatest?

A. $1.25, -3.4, -\frac{15}{4}, -3\frac{7}{9}$

B. $-3\frac{7}{9}, -\frac{15}{4}, -3.4, 1.25$

C. $-\frac{15}{4}, -3\frac{7}{9}, -3.4, 1.25$

D. $-3\frac{7}{9}, -\frac{15}{4}, 1.25, -3.4$

SHOW YOUR WORK!

Test B Name: ____________________

Directions: Read each problem carefully and select the best answer.

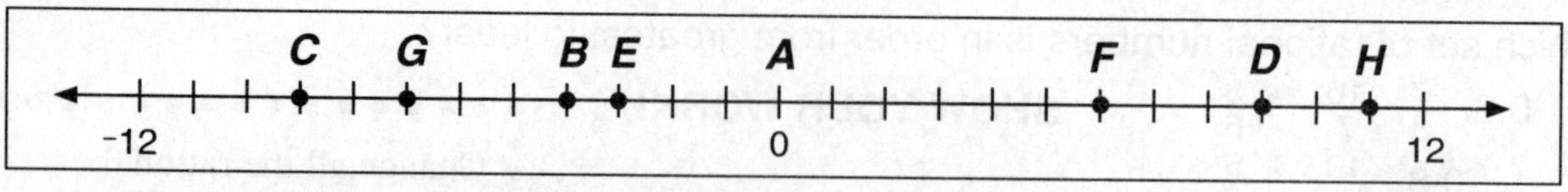

Use the number line to answer questions 61 and 62.

61. Which set of numbers shows the integer naming point *H* on the number line followed by its absolute value?

A. 11 and -11

B. -11 and -11

C. -11 and 11

D. 11 and 11

Use what you know! Integers are the counting numbers, their opposites, and zero. Absolute value is always positive.

62. Which set of numbers shows the integer naming point *C* on the number line followed by its absolute value?

A. 9 and 9

B. -9 and -9

C. -9 and 9

D. 9 and -9

63. Mount McKinley in Alaska is 20,320 feet above sea level. Write an integer to represent 20,320 feet above sea level and the absolute value of that integer.

A. 20,320 and 20,320

B. -20,320 and 20,320

C. 20,320 and -20,320

D. -20,320 and -20,320

Think about it! *Above sea level* suggests a positive number.

64. New Orleans is 8 feet below sea level. Write an integer to represent 8 feet below sea level and the absolute value of that integer.

A. -8 and -8

B. 8 and -8

C. -8 and 8

D. 8 and 8

Test B **Name:** ______________________

Directions: Read each problem carefully and select the best answer.

65. Which product best represents the exponential expression?

7^3

A. 7×3

B. $3 \times 3 \times 3 \times 3 \times 3 \times 3 \times 3$

C. $7 \times 7 \times 7$

D. none of the above

Think about it. Which number should be used as the base (number being multiplied)?

66. Evaluate the exponential expression.

7^3

A. 10

B. 21

C. 2,187

D. 343

SHOW YOUR WORK!

The exponent tells you how many times to use the base as a factor.

67. Which product best represents the exponential expression?

5^4

A. $5 \times 5 \times 5 \times 5$

B. 5×4

C. $4 \times 4 \times 4 \times 4 \times 4$

D. none of the above

68. Evaluate the exponential expression.

5^4

A. 20

B. 625

C. 1,024

D. 9

SHOW YOUR WORK!

Test B Name: ______________________

Directions: Read each problem carefully and select the algebraic expression that best represents the given word expression.

69. 16 decreased by a number x

A. $x - 16$

B. $16 - x$

C. $16 + x$

D. $16 \div x$

70. the quotient of a number c divided by 2

The *quotient* is the answer to a division problem.

A. $2 \div c$

B. $c - 2$

C. $c + 2$

D. $c \div 2$

71. the product of 9 and a number h

The *product* is the answer to a multiplication problem.

A. $9h$

B. $9 + h$

C. $9 - h$

D. $9 \div h$

72. 12 more than a number b

A. $12b$

B. $12 \div b$

C. $12 + b$

D. $12 - b$

Test B Name: ____________________

Directions: Read each problem carefully and select the best answer.

73. Evaluate the expression for $n = 2$.

$n^4 + 3(3) + 3n$

SHOW YOUR WORK!

Pay close attention to the operation signs in the expression and follow the order of operations.

A. 23
B. 31
C. 120
D. none of the above

74. Evaluate the expression for $x = 4$.

$x^3 - 3(5) + x \div 4$

SHOW YOUR WORK!

Using an exponent is a convenient way to multiply a number by itself.

A. 4
B. 306
C. 50
D. none of the above

75. Use the expression $2p + 4p + 2$ to find how many points Seeta earned at Saturday's track meet. She earned 3 points for each of the two relay races she competed in and 3 points for each of the four 50-metre dashes she competed in. Seeta also received 2 points for being voted the outstanding new athlete in Saturday's track events. Hint: $p = 3$.

SHOW YOUR WORK!

A. 20 points
B. 8 points
C. 18 points
D. none of the above

76. Use the expression $2m + 10$ to find how many miles Satish drove his car today. He drove 30 miles to work and the same number of miles back home from work. During his lunch time, he drove 10 miles round trip to get food. During his break, he rode with his friend 8 miles round trip to the bank and back to work. Hint: $m = 30$.

SHOW YOUR WORK!

A. 60 miles
B. 48 miles
C. 78 miles
D. 70 miles

Test B **Name:** ____________________

Directions: Use the distributive property to find an equivalent expression.

77. $8(9x + 9)$

A. $72x + 17$
B. $72x + 9$
C. $72x + 72$
D. $72 + 72$

SHOW YOUR WORK!

78. $6(7 + 5y)$

A. $42 + 30$
B. $42 + 30y$
C. $42 + 5y$
D. $7 + 30y$

SHOW YOUR WORK!

Multiply each term inside the parentheses by 6.

79. $49j + 42$

A. $7(7j + 6j)$
B. $91j$
C. $7(7 + 6)$
D. $7(7j + 6)$

SHOW YOUR WORK!

For each answer choice, multiply the terms inside the parentheses by the term outside the parentheses; which one matches the given expression?

80. $12g + 36$

A. $48g$
B. $3(4 + 12)$
C. $12(g + 3)$
D. $12(g + 3g)$

SHOW YOUR WORK!

Test B Name: ______________

Directions: Read each problem carefully and select the best answer.

81. Which value, when substituted for y, makes the inequality true?

$(y + 6) \times 4 < 40$

A. 5
B. 4
C. 2
D. 7

SHOW YOUR WORK!

Substitute each given value in place of *y* in the inequality to find which value makes it true.

82. Which value, when substituted for w, makes the equation true?

$w - (3 \times 3) = 37$

A. 46
B. 31
C. 28
D. 40

SHOW YOUR WORK!

83. Which open sentence is true when $a = 7$?

A. $a + (4 \times 5) > 29$
B. $41 - 3a = 17$
C. $6a + (3 \times 2) = 72$
D. $(72 \div 8) - a = 2$

SHOW YOUR WORK!

Replace *a* with 7 in each open sentence and solve using the order of operations.

84. Which open sentence is true when $z = 9$?

A. $(45 \div z) + 6 = 3 \times 5$
B. $4z - 8 = 28$
C. $2 + 7z = 58$
D. $z + 82 - 3 < 79$

SHOW YOUR WORK!

Test B Name: ______________________

Directions: Read each problem carefully and select the best answer.

85. Find the area of the parallelogram.

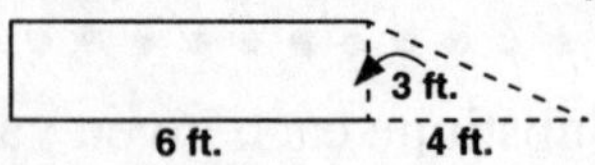

A. 9 ft.^{2}
B. 18 ft.^{2}
C. 6 ft.^{2}
D. 18 ft.

SHOW YOUR WORK!

The parallelogram is the part of the figure that has two sets of parallel sides.

86. Find the area of the trapezoid.

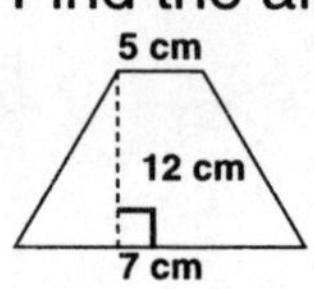

A. 72 in.^{2}
B. 144 cm^2
C. 12 cm^2
D. 72 cm^2

SHOW YOUR WORK!

87. Find the area of the triangle.

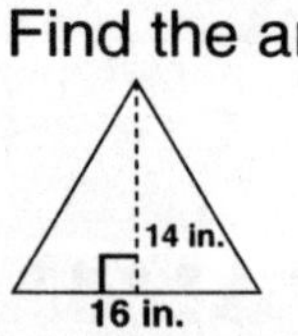

A. 112 in.
B. 224 in.^{2}
C. 112 in.^{2}
D. 15 in.^{2}

SHOW YOUR WORK!

Remember the formula for finding the area of a triangle: $A = \frac{1}{2} bh$.

88. Find the area of the triangle.

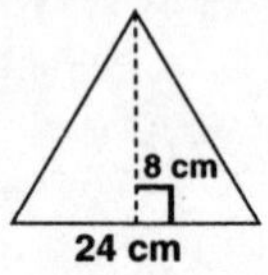

A. 192 cm^2
B. 16 cm
C. 96 cm^2
D. 96 cm

SHOW YOUR WORK!

Test B Name: ____________________

Directions: Read each problem carefully and select the best answer.

89. Find the volume of the rectangular prism.

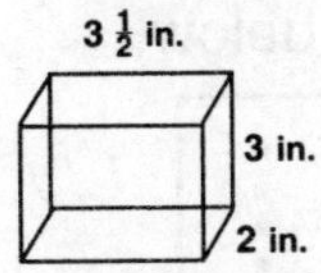

A. $8\frac{1}{2}$ in.^{3}
B. 21 in.^{2}
C. 24 in.^{3}
D. 21 in.^{3}

SHOW YOUR WORK!

Use what you know! Volume is measured in cubic units.

90. Find the volume of the rectangular prism.

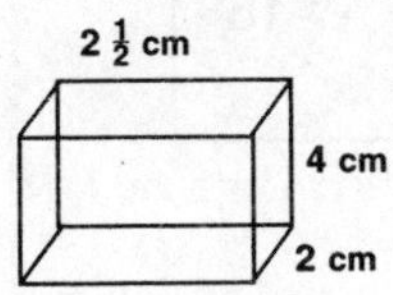

A. 20 cm^2
B. 16 cm^3
C. 20 cm^3
D. $8\frac{1}{2}$ cm^3

SHOW YOUR WORK!

Remember to convert mixed numbers to improper fractions before multiplying.

91. Find the volume of the rectangular prism.

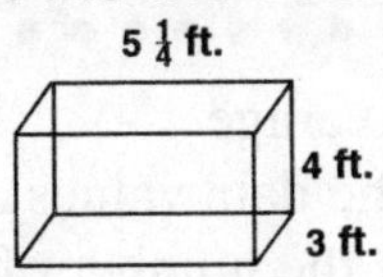

A. $12\frac{1}{4}$ ft.^{3}
B. 63 ft.^{3}
C. 60 ft.^{3}
D. 63 ft.^{2}

SHOW YOUR WORK!

92. Find the volume of the rectangular prism.

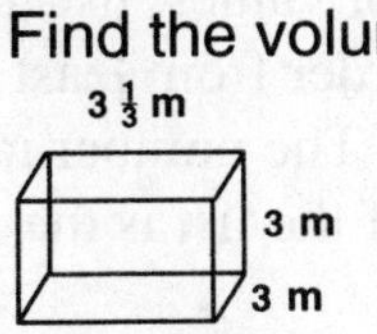

A. 30 m^2
B. 9 m^3
C. $9\frac{1}{3}$ m^3
D. 30 m^3

SHOW YOUR WORK!

Test B Name: ____________________

Directions: Read each problem carefully and select the best answer.

Nitin wanted to find out the number of hours per week his classmates worked on their homework. He took a survey and recorded the results on the dot plot below.

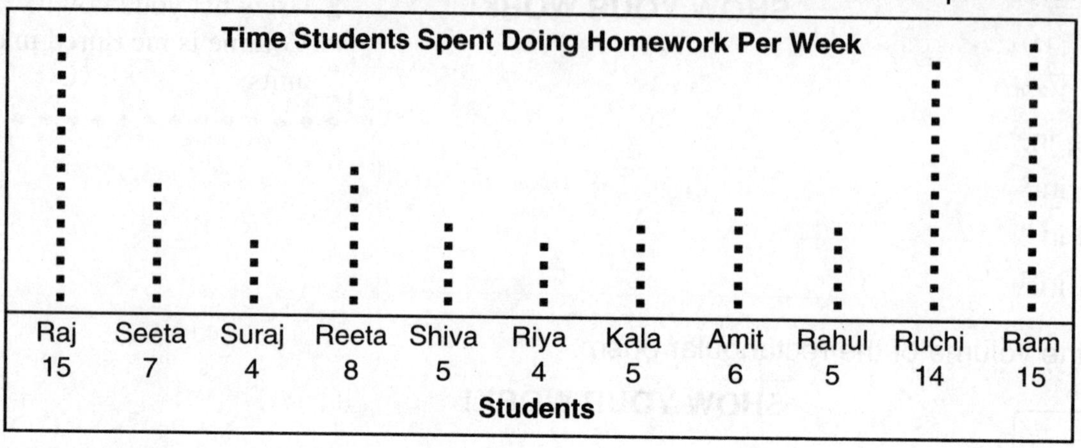

Use the dot plot to answer the questions.

93. What is the total number of hours spent doing homework per week?

A. 80 hours
B. 84 hours
C. 88 hours
D. 11 hours

SHOW YOUR WORK!

94. What is the mean number of hours spent studying?

A. 8 classmates
B. 88 hours
C. 6 hours
D. 8 hours

SHOW YOUR WORK!

mean = average
Add all the data values and divide by the number of values that were added.

95. What is the median number of hours spent studying?

A. 5 hours
B. 6 hours
C. 4 hours
D. 8 hours

SHOW YOUR WORK!

To find the median of an odd number of values, list the data in order from least to greatest. The number in the middle of the list is the median.

96. How is the data on the dot plot distributed?

A. spread out to the right
B. spread out to the left
C. no noticeable shape
D. symmetrically

Test B Name: ____________________

Directions: Read each problem carefully and select the best answer.

A dentist wanted to see how long her patients' wait times were. She recorded the data and created the histogram below.

97. Which wait time is an outlier on the histogram?

A. 1 to 5 minutes
B. 26 to 30 minutes
C. 36 to 40 minutes
D. 41 to 45 minutes

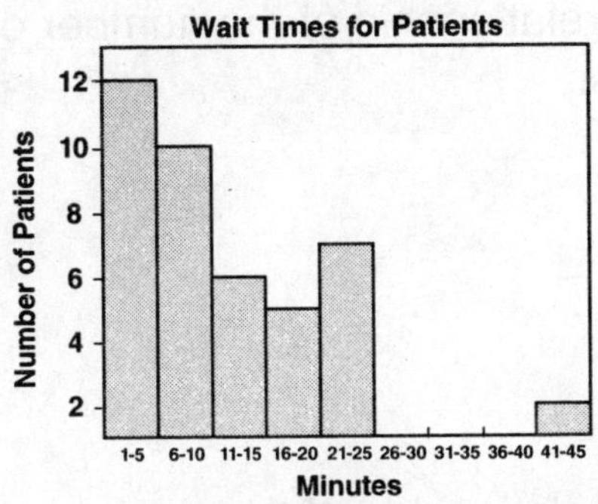

Outliers are data points that lie away from other data on the histogram.

Use the box plot and the list of values to answer questions 98–100.

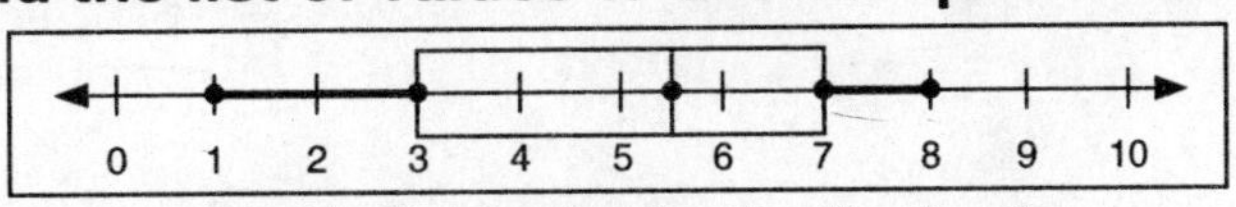

7, 1, 5, 8, 7, 3, 2, 8, 3, 6

98. What is the median of the data shown in the box plot?

A. 5
B. 6
C. 5.5
D. 5 and 6

SHOW YOUR WORK!

99. What is the mean absolute deviation?

A. 2.2
B. 22
C. 5
D. 5.5

SHOW YOUR WORK!

Find the mean of the ten data values given. Then find the difference between that mean and each number in the list. Finally, find the mean of the differences that you just calculated.

100. What is the interquartile range?

A. 7
B. 4
C. 6
D. 1

SHOW YOUR WORK!

Test C Name: ____________________

Directions: Read each problem carefully and select the best answer.

□ △ △ ○ ○ ○ □ ○ ○ △ ○ △

Use the picture to answer questions 1 and 20.

1. Which three ratios show the relationship of the number of squares to the number of triangles?
   - **A.** 4:2, $\frac{4}{2}$, 4 to 2
   - **B.** 2:6, $\frac{2}{6}$, 2 to 6
   - **C.** 2:4, $\frac{2}{4}$, 2 to 4
   - **D.** 2:12, $\frac{2}{12}$, 2 to 12

2. Which three ratios show the relationship of the total number of shapes to the number of circles.
   - **A.** 12:2, $\frac{12}{2}$, 12 to 2
   - **B.** 6:12, $\frac{6}{12}$, 6 to 12
   - **C.** 12:4, $\frac{12}{4}$, 12 to 4
   - **D.** 12:6, $\frac{12}{6}$, 12 to 6

3. Satish is having a pizza party. He ordered 2 cheese pizzas, 4 pepperoni pizzas, 3 meat lover's pizzas, and 1 vegetarian pizza. What is the ratio of meat lover's pizzas to the total number of pizzas ordered?
   - **A.** 3:1
   - **B.** 3:10
   - **C.** 3:2
   - **D.** 10:3

   SHOW YOUR WORK!

4. Karan and Kiran decided to make beaded bracelets to sell at the county fair in July. They decided each bracelet should have 14 blue beads, 16 red beads, and 15 white beads. What is the ratio of red beads to blue beads on the bracelets?
   - **A.** 16:14
   - **B.** 14:16
   - **C.** 16:15
   - **D.** 16:45

Test C Name: ____________________

Directions: Read each problem carefully and select the best answer.

5. Complete the ratio table.

A. 23
B. 28
C. 36
D. 32

8	6
16	12
24	18
	24
40	30

6. Complete the ratio table.

A. 11
B. 13
C. 12
D. 14

6	4
12	8
18	
24	16
30	20

7. Ferheena just got her first car. The car dealer told her that she would be able to drive 120 kilometres on the 8 gallons of petrol he put in her car. At this rate, how many gallons of petrol will it take for her drive 600 kilometres? Use the ratio table to help you solve the problem or to check your answer.

A. 15 gallons
B. 9,000 gallons
C. 12 gallons
D. 40 gallons

Kilometres	Gallons

8. The Gupta family decided to go to the park even though it was a long ride. Karan and Satish decided to count the number of white cars they passed along the way. They counted 8 white cars in 6 minutes. At this rate, how many white cars will they pass in 30 minutes?

A. 30 white cars
B. 40 white cars
C 80 white cars
D. 12 white cars

White Cars	Minutes

Test C **Name:** ______________________

Directions: Read each problem carefully and select the best answer.

9. Find the rate and unit rate given the following information: ₹7.92 for 6 pieces.

A. rate = $\frac{\text{₹}7.92}{6\text{ pieces}}$; unit rate = $\frac{\text{₹}1.36}{6\text{ pieces}}$

B. rate = $\frac{\text{₹}7.92}{6\text{ pieces}}$; unit rate = $\frac{\text{₹}1.32}{6\text{ pieces}}$

C. rate = $\frac{\text{₹}7.92}{6\text{ pieces}}$; unit rate = $\frac{\text{₹}1.32}{1\text{ piece}}$

D. none of the above

SHOW YOUR WORK!

10. Find the rate and unit rate given the following information: 48 roses for 6 vases.

A. rate = $\frac{6\text{ vases}}{48\text{ roses}}$; unit rate = $\frac{0.125\text{ vase}}{1\text{ rose}}$

B. rate = $\frac{48\text{ roses}}{6\text{ vases}}$; unit rate = $\frac{8\text{ roses}}{6\text{ vases}}$

C. rate = $\frac{48\text{ roses}}{6\text{ vases}}$; unit rate = $\frac{7\text{ roses}}{1\text{ vase}}$

D. rate = $\frac{48\text{ roses}}{6\text{ vases}}$; unit rate = $\frac{8\text{ roses}}{1\text{ vase}}$

SHOW YOUR WORK!

11. Naveen participated in 28 bike races over a 7-week period. If he participated in the same number of races each week, how many races did he participate in each week?

A. $\frac{4\text{ races}}{7\text{ weeks}}$

B. $\frac{4\text{ races}}{1\text{ week}}$

C. $\frac{3\text{ races}}{1\text{ week}}$

D. $\frac{0.25\text{ week}}{1\text{ race}}$

SHOW YOUR WORK!

12. Kala typed 1,200 words in 20 minutes on her computer keyboard. At this rate, how many words can she type per minute?

A. 600 words per minute

B. 24,000 words per minute

C. 60 words per minute

D. 20 words per minute

SHOW YOUR WORK!

Test C Name: ______________

Directions: Read each problem carefully and select the best answer.

13. Change the percent to a fraction to find 30% of 200.

A. 600
B. 6
C. 60
D. 30

SHOW YOUR WORK!

14. Change the percent to a fraction to find 55% of 500.

A. $27\frac{1}{2}$
B. 275
C. 250
D. 2,750

SHOW YOUR WORK!

15. Aanand has a membership card to get 20% off the cost of plants at the Township Garden Center. The regular price of a rose bush is ₹36.50. How much money will Aanand save when he buys a rose bush?

A. ₹73
B. ₹29.20
C. ₹0.73
D. ₹7.30

SHOW YOUR WORK!

16. Nitin's train ride to and from work each day adds 25% more time to his normal workday of eight hours. How much time does Nitin spend riding to and from work on the train each day?

A. 2 hours
B. 10 hours
C. 32 hours
D. $\frac{1}{5}$ of an hour

SHOW YOUR WORK!

Test C Name: ____________________

Directions: Read each problem carefully and select the best answer. Answers must be in simplest form.

17. Find the quotient.

$\frac{1}{3} \div \frac{5}{9}$

A. $\frac{9}{15}$
B. $\frac{5}{27}$
C. $1\frac{2}{3}$
D. $\frac{3}{5}$

SHOW YOUR WORK!

18. Divide.

$\frac{2}{5} \div \frac{2}{3}$

A. $1\frac{2}{3}$
B. $\frac{3}{5}$
C. $\frac{4}{15}$
D. $\frac{6}{10}$

SHOW YOUR WORK!

19. Raju has $\frac{3}{4}$ acre of land. He wants to divide the land into $\frac{1}{8}$-acre parcels. How many $\frac{1}{8}$-acre parcels of land will he have?

A. $\frac{24}{4}$ parcels
B. $\frac{3}{32}$ parcel
C. 6 parcels
D. $\frac{1}{6}$ parcel

SHOW YOUR WORK!

20. Raj made $\frac{3}{4}$ of a litre of homemade tomato sauce. How many $\frac{1}{3}$-litre servings of sauce did he make?

A. $2\frac{1}{4}$ servings
B. $\frac{1}{4}$ serving
C. $\frac{4}{9}$ serving
D. 4 servings

SHOW YOUR WORK!

Test C Name: ______________________

Directions: Read each problem carefully and select the best answer.

21. Divide.

6,885 ÷ 367

A. 279 R18
B. 18 R279
C. 18
D. 17 R279

SHOW YOUR WORK!

22. Find the quotient.

7,346 ÷ 15

A. 489
B. 48 R11
C. 489 R11
D. 488 R26

SHOW YOUR WORK!

23. Simplify.

3,064 ÷ 48

A. 62 R88
B. 63 R4
C. 63
D. 63 R40

SHOW YOUR WORK!

24. The wildlife bird refuge has 9,450 birds. The birds were equally separated into 175 different areas. How many birds are in each area?

A. 54 birds
B. 5 birds R4 birds
C. 53 birds R175 birds
D. 54 areas

SHOW YOUR WORK!

Test C Name: ____________________

Directions: Read each problem carefully and select the best answer.

25. Find the quotient.

66.15 ÷ 0.63

A. 15.0
B. 10.5
C. 105.0
D. 1.05

SHOW YOUR WORK!

26. Find the difference.

6.269 – 0.8

A. 5,469
B. 6.261
C. 0.5469
D. 5.469

SHOW YOUR WORK!

27. Find the sum.

56.1 + 24.742

A. 80.842
B. 8.0842
C. 808.42
D. 25.303

SHOW YOUR WORK!

28. Find the product.

9.17 × 4.33

A. 3970.61
B. 397.061
C. 39.7061
D. 3.97061

SHOW YOUR WORK!

Test C Name: ____________________

Directions: Read each problem carefully and select the best answer.

29. What is the GCF of 21 and 49?

A. 2
B. 7
C. 21
D. 3

SHOW YOUR WORK!

30. What is the greatest common factor of 12 and 36?

A. 4
B. 3
C. 6
D. 12

SHOW YOUR WORK!

31. Which two numbers do not have a GCF of 3?

A. 6 and 21
B. 12 and 63
C. 18 and 42
D. 15 and 24

SHOW YOUR WORK!

32. Which pair of numbers is correctly listed with its GCF?

A. 36 and 48: GCF = 12
B. 8 and 16: GCF = 4
C. 14 and 35: GCF = 5
D. 56 and 64: GCF = 4

SHOW YOUR WORK!

Test C Name: ______________________

Directions: Read each problem carefully and select the best answer.

33. What is the least common multiple (LCM) of 3 and 12?

A. 36
B. 24
C. 12
D. 48

SHOW YOUR WORK!

34. What is the LCM of 5 and 10?

A. 10
B. 35
C. 20
D. 30

SHOW YOUR WORK!

35. Which pair of numbers is correctly listed with its LCM?

A. 3 and 9: LCM = 18
B. 6 and 7: LCM = 84
C. 2 and 8: LCM = 24
D. 8 and 9: LCM = 72

SHOW YOUR WORK!

36. Which pair of numbers has an LCM of 12?

A. 9 and 12
B. 11 and 12
C. 4 and 6
D. 3 and 8

SHOW YOUR WORK!

Test C Name: ____________

Directions: Read each problem carefully and select the best answer.

37. Which expression is equal to 48 + 16?

A. $8(6 \times 2)$
B. $6(8 \times 3)$
C. $(8 \times 6) + (8 \times 2)$
D. $(8 + 6) \times (8 + 2)$

SHOW YOUR WORK!

38. Which expression is equal to 32 + 8?

A. $4(8 \times 2)$
B. $4(8 + 2)$
C. $(4 \times 8) \times (4 \times 2)$
D. $8(4 + 2)$

SHOW YOUR WORK!

39. Which number makes the equation true?

56 + 28 = ___ (8 + 4)

A. 8
B. 6
C. 9
D. 7

SHOW YOUR WORK!

40. Which expression is equal to $(3 \times 7) + (3 \times 6)$?

A. $3(7 \times 6)$
B. 21×18
C. $3(7 + 6)$
D. $7(3 + 6)$

SHOW YOUR WORK!

Test C Name: ____________

Directions: Read each problem carefully and select the best answer.

Narayan compared and recorded the high and low tides of five coastal towns in New Jersey. The results are listed in the table below.

Town	High Tide	Low Tide
Seaside	15 feet above sea level	10 feet below sea level
Spray Beach	26 feet above sea level	5 feet below sea level
Point Pleasant	8 feet above sea level	12 feet below sea level
Atlantic City	31 feet above sea level	1 foot below sea level
Brigantine	7 feet above sea level	7 feet below sea level

41. Which integers show the highest and lowest tides for Spray Beach?

A. highest = -26; lowest = -5

B. highest = -5; lowest = 26

C. highest = 26; lowest = 5

D. highest = 26; lowest = -5

42. Which town had the highest tide?

A. Atlantic City

B. Spray Beach

C. Point Pleasant

D. Seaside

43. Which town's highest and lowest tides are opposite integers?

A. Seaside

B. Brigantine

C. Point Pleasant

D. Atlantic City

44. Which two integers show the highest and lowest tides for Point Pleasant?

A. highest = -12; lowest = 8

B. highest = 8; lowest = 12

C. highest = 8; lowest = -12

D. highest = -8; lowest = 12

Test C   Name: ______________________

Directions: Read each problem carefully and select the best answer.

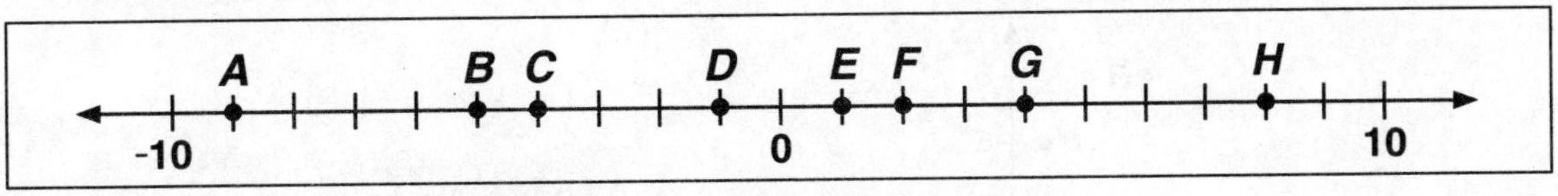

Use the number line to answer questions 45 and 46.

45. Which point on the number line is the opposite of 4?

A. *B*
B. *D*
C. *G*
D. *C*

46. Which point on the number line is the opposite of -1?

A. *F*
B. *E*
C. *A*
D. *H*

47. Where would the opposite of 12 be located on a number line?

A. 12 spaces to the right of 0
B. between 0 and 1
C. 12 spaces to the left of 0
D. between -1 and 0

48. Which integer is equal to -(-6)?

A. (-6)
B. 12
C. 6
D. -6

Test C Name: ______________________

Directions: Read each problem carefully and select the best answer.

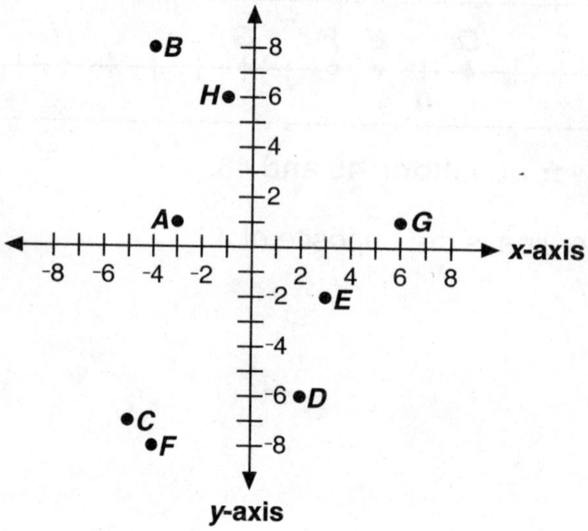

49. Which point is located at (-4,-8)?

A. *B* **C.** *F*

B. *C* **D.** *H*

50. Which point is located at (2,-6)?

A. *D* **C.** *G*

B. *H* **D.** *A*

51. Which ordered pair is located at point ***E***?

A. (6,1) **C.** (-4,8)

B. (3,-2) **D.** (-3,1)

52. Which ordered pair is located at point ***C***?

A. (-1,6) **C.** (-4,-8)

B. (-3,2) **D.** (-5,-7)

Test C **Name:** ____________________

Directions: Read each problem carefully and select the best answer.

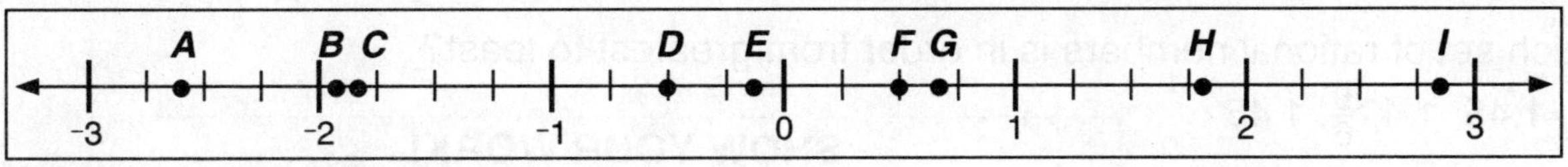

53. Which point is located at $-\frac{5}{10}$?

A. *D*
B. *F*
C. *E*
D. *B*

54. Which point is located at 2.8?

A. *A*
B. *I*
C. *H*
D. *C*

55. Which rational number is located at point *H*?

A. 0.7
B. $-\frac{9}{5}$
C. -1.9
D. $1\frac{4}{5}$

56. Which rational number is located at point *A*?

A. 2.6
B. -1.9
C. -2.6
D. $-\frac{5}{10}$

Test C Name: ______________________

Directions: Read each problem carefully and select the best answer.

57. Which set of rational numbers is in order from greatest to least?

A. $-1.45, 1.4, \frac{5}{6}, 1.45$

B. $-1.45, \frac{5}{6}, 1.4, 1.45$

C. $1.45, \frac{5}{6}, 1.4, -1.45$

D. $1.45, 1.4, \frac{5}{6}, -1.45$

SHOW YOUR WORK!

58. Which set of rational numbers is in order from greatest to least?

A. $-1\frac{5}{8}, -1.6, -\frac{5}{4}, -0.33$

B. $-0.33, -\frac{5}{4}, -1\frac{5}{8}, -1.6$

C. $-0.33, -\frac{5}{4}, -1.6, -1\frac{5}{8}$

D. $-\frac{5}{4}, -0.33, -1.6, -1\frac{5}{8}$

SHOW YOUR WORK!

59. Which set of rational numbers is in order from least to greatest?

A. $2.7, -4.17, 1\frac{2}{5}, -\frac{14}{3}$

B. $-\frac{14}{3}, -4.17, 2.7, 1\frac{2}{5}$

C. $-\frac{14}{3}, -4.17, 1\frac{2}{5}, 2.7$

D. $2.7, 1\frac{2}{5}, -4.17, -\frac{14}{3}$

SHOW YOUR WORK!

60. Which set of rational numbers is in order from least to greatest?

A. $-2.3, -2\frac{1}{9}, -\frac{2}{7}, \frac{2}{7}$

B. $\frac{2}{7}, -\frac{2}{7}, -2\frac{1}{9}, -2.3$

C. $-2.3, -2\frac{1}{9}, \frac{2}{7}, -\frac{2}{7}$

D. $\frac{2}{7}, -2.3, -2\frac{1}{9}, -\frac{2}{7}$

SHOW YOUR WORK!

Test C   Name: ______________________

Directions: Read each problem carefully and select the best answer.

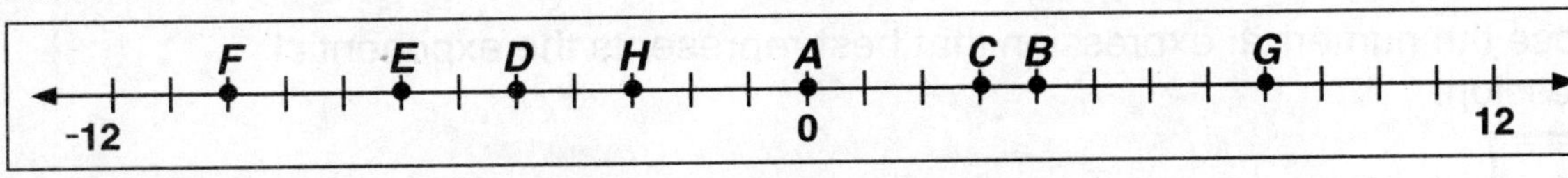

Use the number line to answer questions 61 and 62.

61. Which set of numbers shows the integer naming point *G* on the number line followed by its absolute value?

A. -8 and 8
B. 7 and 7
C. 8 and 8
D. 8 and -8

62. Which set of numbers shows the integer naming point *D* on the number line followed by its absolute value?

A. -4 and 4
B. -5 and -5
C. 5 and 5
D. -5 and 5

63. Prospect Creek Camp in northern Alaska recorded a record low temperature of 80° below zero. Write an integer to represent the temperature and the absolute value of that integer.

A. -80 and 80
B. 80 and -80
C. 80 and 80
D. -80 and -80

64. One of the highest temperatures recorded in the western hemisphere was one hundred thirty-four degrees in Death Valley, California. Write an integer to represent one hundred thirty-four degrees and the absolute value of that integer.

A. -134 and 134
B. 134 and -134
C. -134 and -134
D. 134 and 134

Test C Name: ____________________

Directions: Read each problem carefully and select the best answer.

65. Choose the numerical expression that best represents the exponential expression.

3^5

A. 3×5
B. $5 \times 5 \times 5$
C. $3 \times 3 \times 3 \times 3 \times 3$
D. none of the above

66. Evaluate the exponential expression.

3^5

SHOW YOUR WORK!

A. 125
B. 15
C. 8
D. 243

67. Choose the numerical expression that best represents the exponential expression.

2^6

A. $2 \times 2 \times 2 \times 2 \times 2 \times 2$
B. 2×6
C. 6×6
D. none of the above

68. Evaluate the exponential expression.

2^6

SHOW YOUR WORK!

A. 12
B. 64
C. 36
D. 8

Test C **Name:** ______________________

Directions: Read each problem carefully and select the algebraic expression that best represents the given word expression.

69. a number *n* divided into 26

A. $26n$

B. $26 \div n$

C. $n \div 26$

D. $n + 26$

70. *t* tickets at ₹12 each

A. $12t$

B. $t - 12$

C. $t + 12$

D. $t \div 12$

71. *r* fewer than16

A. $16r$

B. $r \div 16$

C. $r - 16$

D. $16 - r$

72. twice a number *h*

A. $2 + h$

B. $2h$

C. $2 - h$

D. $2 \div h$

Test C Name: ____________________

Directions: Read each problem carefully and select the best answer.

73. Evaluate the expression for $t = 6$.

$$t^2 - 2(2) + t \div 2$$

A. 35
B. 32
C. 11
D. none of the above

SHOW YOUR WORK!

74. Evaluate the expression for $r = 4$.

$$r^3 + 52 \div r$$

A. 25
B. 77
C. 29
D. none of the above

SHOW YOUR WORK!

75. Karan earns ₹55 per day plus tips for babysitting. Last week she worked 5 days and this week she worked 3 days. Each week she received tips totaling ₹25, which she shared with her assistant. Use the expression $8e + 2(25) \div 2$ to determine how much money Karan received for the last two weeks of babysitting. ($e = 55$)

A. ₹490
B. ₹425
C. ₹465
D. ₹5,525

SHOW YOUR WORK!

76. Kala's washing machine broke. The repairman charges ₹65 to come to Kala's home to inspect the machine. He charges ₹35 per hour for his services and it will be another ₹54 to buy the part that needs to be replaced. It took the repairman 3 hours to complete the repairs. Use the expression $65 + 35h + 54$ to determine how much money it will cost Kala to get her washing machine repaired. ($h = 3$).

A. ₹354
B. ₹462
C. ₹170
D. ₹224

SHOW YOUR WORK!

Test C Name: ____________________

Directions: Use the distributive property to find an equivalent expression.

77. $3(5 + 3r)$

A. $15 + 9$
B. $15 + 15r$
C. $15 + 9r$
D. $15 + 3r$

SHOW YOUR WORK!

78. $2(6 + 24k)$

A. $12 + 24k$
B. $12 + 48k$
C. $6 + 48k$
D. $12 + 48$

SHOW YOUR WORK!

79. $8 + 6x$

A. $2(4 + 3x)$
B. $2(4 + 3)$
C. $2(4x + 3x)$
D. $14x$

SHOW YOUR WORK!

80. $12g + 24$

A. $36g$
B. $12(1 + 2)$
C. $12(1 + 2g)$
D. $12(g + 2)$

SHOW YOUR WORK!

Test C

Name: ____________________

Directions: Read each problem carefully and select the best answer.

81. Which value, when substituted for n, makes the equation true?

$$(n \div 6) + 7 = 13$$

A. 12
B. 36
C. 30
D. 6

SHOW YOUR WORK!

82. Which value, when substituted for b, makes the inequality true?

$$3b - (12 \div 2) > 10$$

A. 5
B. 3
C. 4
D. 7

SHOW YOUR WORK!

83. Which open sentence is true when $n = 4$?

A. $(12 \times n) \div 8 = 6$
B. $n + 50 - 23 = 35$
C. $(15 - 5) + (5n) < 6 \times 5$
D. $8n + 16 = 3 \times 14$

SHOW YOUR WORK!

84. Which open sentence is true when $y = 8$?

A. $9 + 6 + (2y) = 29$
B. $46 - y > 6 \times 7$
C. $(5 \times 7) + (64 \div y) = 43$
D. $(y - 3) + (4 \times 9) = 58 - 12$

SHOW YOUR WORK!

Test C **Name:** ____________________

Directions: Read each problem carefully and select the best answer.

85. Find the area of the parallelogram.

A. 60 cm^2
B. 60 ft.
C. 60 $ft.^2$
D. 30 $ft.^2$

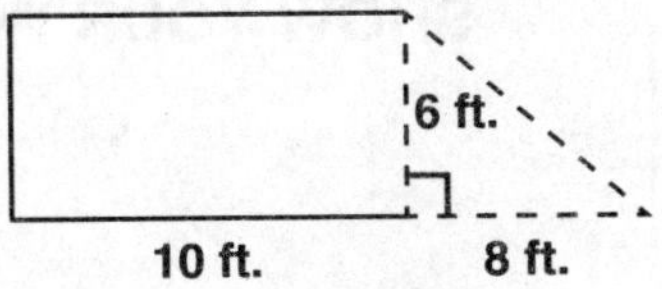

SHOW YOUR WORK!

86. Find the area of the trapezoid.

A. 135 cm
B. 270 cm^2
C. 27 cm^2
D. 135 cm^2

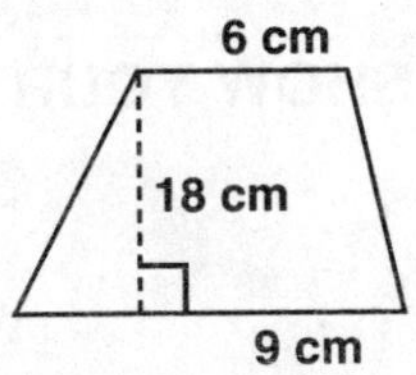

SHOW YOUR WORK!

87. Find the area of the triangle.

A. 12 m
B. 12 m^2
C. 24 m^2
D. 5 m^2

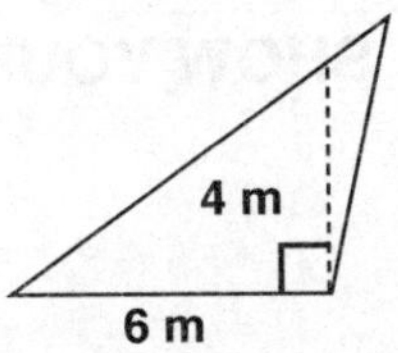

SHOW YOUR WORK!

88. Find the area of the triangle.

A. 154 in.
B. 308 in.
C. 18 $in.^2$
D. 154 $in.^2$

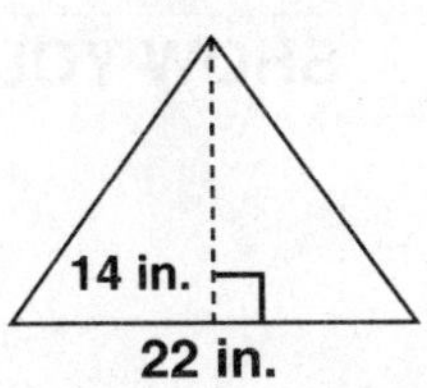

SHOW YOUR WORK!

Test C Name: ____________________

Directions: Read each problem carefully and select the best answer.

89. Find the volume of the rectangular prism.

A. 42 in.^{2}
B. $12\frac{5}{8}$ in.^{3}
C. 42 in.^{3}
D. 40 in.^{3}

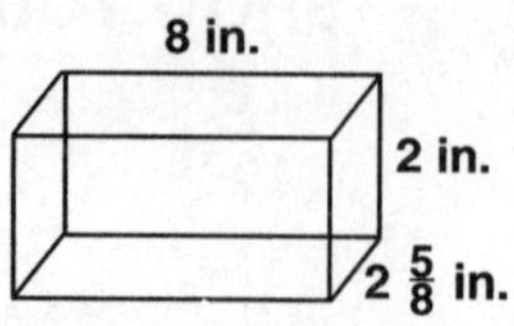

SHOW YOUR WORK!

90. Find the volume of the rectangular prism.

A. $11\frac{3}{4}$ ft.^{3}
B. 60 ft.^{3}
C. 48 ft.^{3}
D. 60 ft.^{2}

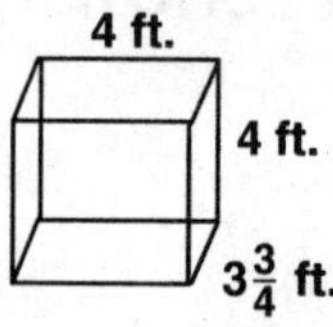

SHOW YOUR WORK!

91. Find the volume of the rectangular prism.

A. 28 ft.^{3}
B. 21 ft.^{3}
C. $9\frac{1}{3}$ ft.^{3}
D. 28 ft.^{2}

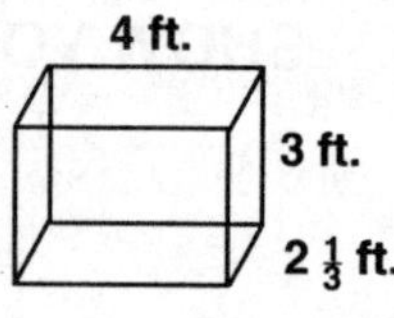

SHOW YOUR WORK!

92. Find the volume of the rectangular prism.

A. 36 m^2
B. $10\frac{1}{4}$ m^3
C. 36 m^3
D. 32 m^3

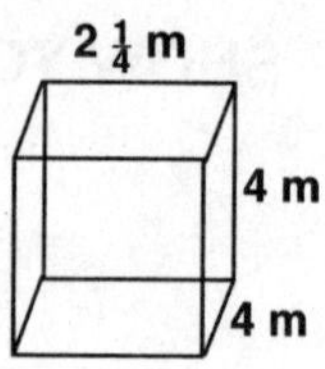

SHOW YOUR WORK!

Test C **Name:** ______________________

Directions: Read each problem carefully and select the best answer.

Rahul and Seema went on a ten-day trip to Africa. They recorded how many lions they saw each day on their trip. The results are shown on the dot plot below.

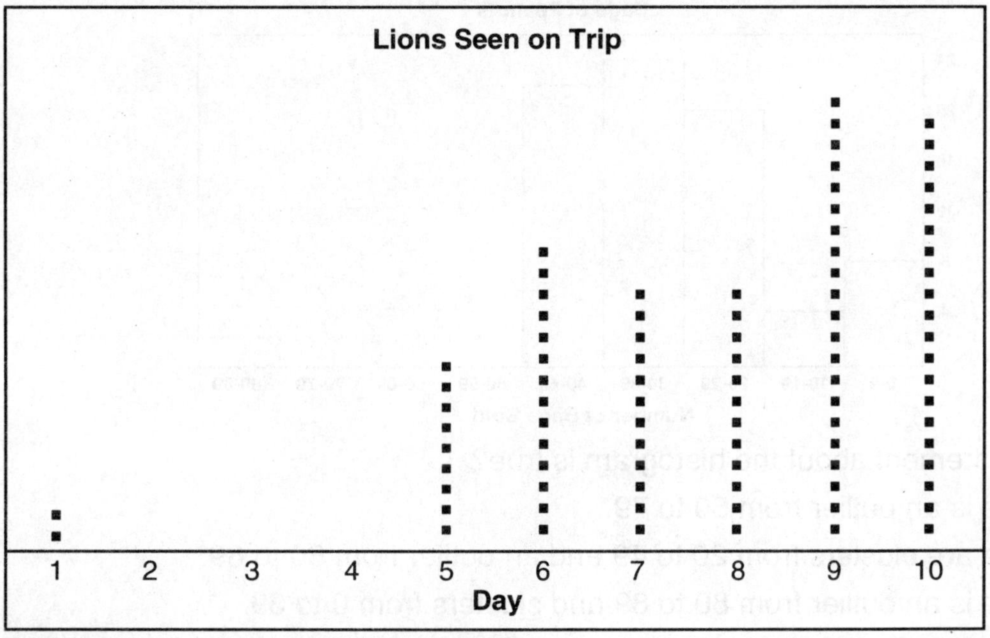

Use the dot plot to answer the questions.

93. What is the total number of lions observed on the trip to Africa?

A. 90 lions **C**. 81 lions

B. 88 lions **D**. 78 lions

SHOW YOUR WORK!

94. What is the mean of the values shown on the dot plot?

A. 10 lions **C.** 9 lions

B. 9 days **D.** 21 lions

SHOW YOUR WORK!

95. What is the median value of the data?

A. 10 **C.** 12

B. 9 and 12 **D.** 10.5

SHOW YOUR WORK!

96. Identify the outlier on the dot plot.

A. Day 9 is the outlier because it has the most dots.

B. Day 1 is the outlier because it is separated from the other data.

C. Days 7 and 8 are outliers because they have the same number of dots.

D. There is no outlier.

Test C Name: ________________

Directions: Read each problem carefully and select the best answer.

Mrs. Verma's 6th graders wanted to sell bags of peanuts to earn money for a class trip. The results of the peanut sale are represented on the histogram below.

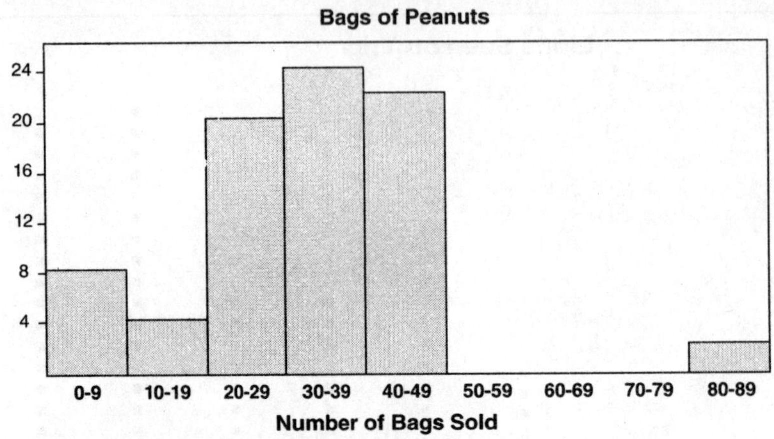

97. Which statement about the histogram is true?

A. There is an outlier from 50 to 79.

B. There are clusters from 20 to 49 and an outlier from 80 to 89.

C. There is an outlier from 80 to 89 and clusters from 0 to 39.

D. The histogram has a symmetric distribution.

Use the box plot and the list of values to answer questions 98–100.

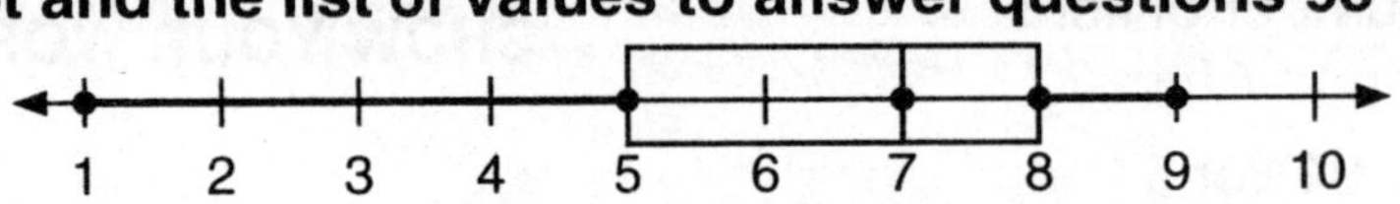

5, 8, 6, 7, 1, 9, 7

98. What is the median value of the box plot?

A. 7 **C.** 5

B. 6 **D.** 9

SHOW YOUR WORK!

99. What is the mean absolute deviation of the data (to the nearest whole number)?

A. 6 **C.** 43

B. 7 **D.** 2

SHOW YOUR WORK!

100. What is the interquartile range?

A. 1 **C.** 3

B. 8 **D.** 9

SHOW YOUR WORK!

Master Answer Sheet

Answers for Test A (pages 10–34)

1. B	11. B	21. C	31. C	41. C	51. A	61. A	71. D	81. D	91. D
2. A	12. C	22. A	32. B	42. D	52. B	62. C	72. B	82. B	92. D
3. C	13. A	23. B	33. C	43. A	53. B	63. D	73. C	83. C	93. B
4. B&D	14. C	24. D	34. A	44. B	54. C	64. C	74. A	84. C	94. C
5. D	15. C	25. B	35. C	45. B	55. D	65. B	75. D	85. A	95. A
6. A	16. B	26. D	36. B	46. D	56. B	66. D	76. B	86. D	96. D
7. C	17. C	27. A	37. B	47. C	57. D	67. B	77. B	87. C	97. C
8. B	18. D	28. C	38. D	48. A	58. B	68. C	78. A	88. D	98. A
9. A	19. B	29. D	39. A	49. D	59. A	69. C	79. C	89. B	99. D
10. D	20. A	30. B	40. B	50. C	60. C	70. A	80. B	90. A	100. B

Answers for Test B (pages 35–59)

1. D	11. B	21. A	31. D	41. B	51. D	61. D	71. A	81. C	91. B
2. C	12. C	22. D	32. C	42. C	52. A	62. C	72. C	82. A	92. D
3. B	13. D	23. B	33. D	43. C	53. D	63. A	73. B	83. D	93. C
4. C	14. A	24. B	34. B	44. A	54. D	64. C	74. C	84. B	94. D
5. C	15. B	25. A	35. C	45. C	55. A	65. C	75. A	85. B	95. B
6. B	16. C	26. B	36. A	46. A	56. B	66. D	76. D	86. D	96. C
7. D	17. B	27. B	37. D	47. D	57. A	67. A	77. C	87. C	97. D
8. B	18. C	28. A	38. A	48. B	58. C	68. B	78. B	88. C	98. C
9. A	19. D	29. A	39. A	49. B	59. D	69. B	79. D	89. D	99. A
10. C	20. C	30. C	40. B	50. B	60. B	70. D	80. C	90. C	100. B

Answers for Test C (pages 60–84)

1. C	11. B	21. B	31. C	41. D	51. B	61. C	71. D	81. B	91. A
2. D	12. C	22. C	32. A	42. A	52. D	62. D	72. B	82. D	92. C
3. B	13. C	23. D	33. C	43. B	53. A	63. A	73. A	83. A	93. A
4. A	14. B	24. A	34. A	44. C	54. B	64. D	74. B	84. C	94. C
5. D	15. D	25. C	35. D	45. D	55. D	65. C	75. C	85. C	95. D
6. C	16. A	26. D	36. C	46. B	56. C	66. D	76. D	86. D	96. B
7. D	17. D	27. A	37. C	47. C	57. D	67. A	77. C	87. B	97. B
8. B	18. B	28. C	38. B	48. C	58. C	68. B	78. B	88. D	98. A
9. C	19. C	29. B	39. D	49. C	59. C	69. B	79. A	89. C	99. D
10. D	20. A	30. D	40. C	50. A	60. A	70. A	80. D	90. B	100. C

Explanations for Test A Answers

Ratios (page 10)

1. **Correct Answer: B**

   There are 2 triangles and 9 shapes in all; the ratio of triangles to total shapes can be written 2:9, $\frac{2}{9}$, or 2 to 9.

   Incorrect Answers:

   A. 2:4, $\frac{2}{4}$, and 2 to 4 represent the ratio of triangles to circles.

   C. The numbers were written in the wrong order; 9:2, $\frac{9}{2}$, and 9 to 2 represent the ratio of the total number of shapes to triangles.

   D. 2:3, $\frac{2}{3}$, and 2 to 3 represent the ratio of triangles to squares.

2. **Correct Answer: A**

   There are 4 circles and 3 squares; the ratio of circles to squares can be written 4:3, $\frac{4}{3}$, or 4 to 3.

   Incorrect Answers:

   B. The numbers were written in the wrong order; 3:4, $\frac{3}{4}$, and 3 to 4 represent the ratio of squares to circles.

   C. 4:9, $\frac{4}{9}$, and 4 to 9 represent the ratio of circles to the total number of shapes.

   D. 3 to 4 is written incorrectly; it represents the ratio of squares to circles.

3. **Correct Answer: C**

   Compare the number of boys (14) to the number of girls (10) to find the ratio of boys to girls (14:10, $\frac{14}{10}$, 14 to 10).

   Incorrect Answers:

   A. The numbers were written in the wrong order; 10:14 represents the ratio of girls to boys.

   B. The numbers were written in the wrong order; $\frac{10}{14}$ represents the ratio of girls to boys.

   D. The numbers were written in the wrong order; 10 to 14 represents the ratio of girls to boys.

4. **Correct Answers: B & D**

   3:5 and $\frac{3}{5}$ is the ratio of rows of tomatoes in Naveen's garden to the number of rows of watermelon in his garden.

   Incorrect Answers:

   A. 5 to 3 is the ratio of rows of watermelon to rows of tomatoes.

   C. 5:3 is the ratio of rows of watermelon to rows of tomatoes.

Ratio Relationships (page 11)

5. **Correct Answer: D**

   Start with the ratio 9:3. Rewrite the ratio as a fraction: $\frac{9}{3}$. Since $9 \times 4 = 36$, multiply the numerator and denominator of the fraction by 4 to complete the ratio table: $\frac{9}{3} = \frac{36}{12}$.

   Incorrect Answers:

   A. 4 was added to the previous number in the column (9).

   B. 4 was subtracted from the next number in the column (15).

   C. The numbers were transposed when recording the answer.

6. **Correct Answer: A**

   Start with the ratio 7:5. Rewrite the ratio as a fraction: $\frac{7}{5}$. Since $5 \times 3 = 15$, multiply the numerator and denominator of the fraction by 3 to complete the ratio table: $\frac{7}{5} = \frac{21}{15}$.

   Incorrect Answers:

   B. The numbers were transposed when recording the answer.

   C. 3 was added to the previous number in the column (14).

   D. 3 was subtracted from the next number in the column (28).

7. **Correct Answer: C**

   Find an equivalent ratio for $\frac{15}{2}$ that has a numerator of 60. Since $15 \times 4 = 60$, multiply 2×4 to get 8: $\frac{15}{2} = \frac{60}{8}$.

   Incorrect Answers:

   A. $\frac{15}{2}$ was multiplied by $\frac{3}{3}$ instead of $\frac{4}{4}$.

   B. 15 was divided by 2 instead of multiplied by 4.

   D. 15 was multiplied by 2 instead of 4.

8. **Correct Answer: B**

   The ratio of lemonade to water is $\frac{2}{4}$. To find an equivalent fraction with a numerator of 10 (10 packets of lemonade), multiply the numerator and denominator by 5: $\frac{2}{4} = \frac{10}{20}$.

   Incorrect Answers:

   A. 2 was multiplied by 4, instead of finding an equivalent fraction for $\frac{2}{4}$.

   C. 4 was added to 5 instead of being multiplied by it.

   D. 12 quarts of water was calculated by adding 1 quart of water for each additional packet of lemonade (after starting with 2 packets of lemonade and 4 quarts of water).

Unit Rate Ratios (page 12)

9. **Correct Answer: A**

   Write the number of miles over the number of hours to find the rate of travel: $\frac{600 \text{ miles}}{12 \text{ hours}}$. The fraction bar indicates division, so divide the number of miles (600) by the number of hours (12) to find the unit rate: $\frac{50 \text{ miles}}{1 \text{ hour}}$. The second number of a unit rate is always 1.

   Incorrect Answers:

   B. The values were reversed when writing the rate, so the unit rate is also incorrect.

   C. When finding the unit rate, the numerator of the rate (600) was correctly divided by 12, but the denominator was not changed to 1.

   D. The values were reversed when writing the rate.

10. **Correct Answer: D**

    Write the cost over the number of kilograms to find the rate: $\frac{₹48}{6 \text{ kilograms}}$. The fraction bar indicates division, so divide the cost

    (₹48) by the number of kilograms (6) to find the unit rate: $\frac{₹8}{1}$ kilogram. The second number of the unit rate is always 1.

    Incorrect Answers:

    A. The values were reversed when writing the rate, so the unit rate is also incorrect.

    B. When finding the unit rate, the numerator of the rate (48) was correctly divided by 6, but the denominator was not changed to 1.

    C. The rate was written incorrectly.

11. **Correct Answer: B**

    Find the unit rate: $\frac{145 \text{ kilometres}}{5 \text{ hours}} = 29$ kilometres per hour. Multiply the unit rate ($\frac{29 \text{ kilometres}}{1 \text{ hour}}$) by the number of hours driven (8) to find how many kilometres Nitin will drive in 8 hours (232 kilometres).

    Incorrect Answers:

    A. 3 was added to 5 hours to get 8 hours, and 3 was added to 145 kilometres to get 148 kilometres.

    C. $\frac{29 \text{ kilometres}}{1 \text{ hour}}$ was multiplied by 3 hours instead of by 8 hours of driving.

    D. The unit rate was incorrectly calculated as $\frac{145 \text{ kilometres}}{8 \text{ hours}}$ =18.125 miles per hour; 18.125 kilometres per hour × 8 hours = 145 kilometres.

Explanations for Test A Answers *(cont.)*

12. Correct Answer: C
Find the unit rate: $\frac{24 \text{ eggs}}{4 \text{ days}}$ = 6 eggs per day. Multiply the unit rate (6 eggs per day) by the number of days (7) to find how many eggs the hen will lay in 7 days (42 eggs).
Incorrect Answers:
A. 6 eggs per day was multiplied by 3 days instead of 7 days.
B. 6 eggs per day is the unit rate; 6 eggs per day was not multiplied by 7 days.
D. The unit rate was incorrectly calculated: $\frac{24 \text{ eggs}}{4 \text{ days}} \neq 8$ eggs per day; 8 eggs per day × 7 days = 56 eggs.

Percent (page 13)

13. Correct Answer: A
4% = $\frac{4}{100}$. *Of* means *multiply:* $\frac{4}{100} \times \frac{250}{1} = \frac{1,000}{100} = 10$.
Incorrect Answers:
B. 4% was incorrectly converted to $\frac{40}{100}$ instead of $\frac{4}{100}$.
C. 4% was incorrectly converted to 4: 4 × 250 = 1,000
D. 4% was incorrectly converted to 4, and the wrong operation (division) was used. 250 ÷ 4 = 62.5 or 62 $\frac{1}{2}$

14. Correct Answer: C
48% = $\frac{48}{100}$. *Of* means *multiply:* $\frac{48}{100} \times \frac{300}{1}$. Cross-cancel 100 and 300 to get $\frac{48}{1} \times \frac{3}{1} = \frac{144}{1} = 144$.
Incorrect Answers:
A. 48% was incorrectly converted to 48: 48 × 300 = 14,000.
B. 48% was incorrectly written as $\frac{100}{48}$, and 300 was incorrectly converted to $\frac{1}{300}$.
D. 48% was incorrectly converted to $\frac{48}{1,000}$.

15. Correct Answer: C
15% = $\frac{15}{100}$ = .15. Multiply to find 15% *of* the bill:
.15 × 35.40 = ₹5.31.
Incorrect Answers:
A. The wrong question was answered: the tip was correctly calculated, but then it was added to the amount of the bill.
B. 15% was incorrectly converted to 15.
D. 15% was incorrectly converted to 1.5 or 15/10.

16. Correct Answer: B
20% = $\frac{20}{100}$. *Of* means *multiply*: $\frac{20}{100} \times \frac{60}{1} = \frac{1,200}{100} = 12$.
Incorrect Answers:
A. 48 kilograms is the amount of lasagna that was sold.
C. 20% was incorrectly written as 20, and the wrong operation (division) was used.
D. 60 kilograms of lasagna was divided by 2.

Dividing Fractions (page 14)

17. Correct Answer: C
Change division to multiplication, and change the divisor to its reciprocal: $\frac{5}{6} \times \frac{10}{6} = \frac{50}{36} = 1\frac{14}{36} = 1\frac{7}{18}$.
Incorrect Answers:
A. Division was changed to multiplication, but the divisor was not changed to its reciprocal.
B. The dividend was changed to its reciprocal instead of the divisor.
D. The answer was not simplified completely.

18. Correct Answer: D
Change division to multiplication, and change the divisor to its reciprocal: $\frac{4}{7} \times \frac{4}{3} = \frac{16}{21}$.
Incorrect Answers:
A. The dividend was changed to its reciprocal instead of the divisor.
B. Division was changed to multiplication, but the divisor was not changed to its reciprocal.
C. A multiplication error occurred: $\frac{4}{7} \times \frac{4}{3} \neq \frac{12}{21}$.

19. Correct Answer: B
Divide the total amount of cheese by $\frac{2}{10}$ kilogram per serving to find how many servings of cheese Reeta has: $\frac{4}{5} \div \frac{2}{10} = \frac{4}{5} \times \frac{10}{2} = \frac{40}{10} = 4$.
Incorrect Answers:
A. Division was changed to multiplication, but the divisor was not changed to its reciprocal.
C. The dividend was changed to its reciprocal instead of the divisor.
D. The answer was not simplified completely.

20. Correct Answer: A
Divide $\frac{8}{12}$ metres (total amount of material) by $\frac{1}{3}$ metre (size of the pieces to be cut) to find how many pieces of material Geeta can make: $\frac{8}{12} \div \frac{1}{3} = \frac{8}{12} \times \frac{3}{1} = \frac{24}{12} = 2$.
Incorrect Answers:
B. Division was changed to multiplication, but the divisor was not changed to its reciprocal.
C. The answer was not simplified completely.
D. The dividend was changed to its reciprocal instead of the divisor.

Dividing Multi-digit Numbers (page 15)

21. Correct Answer: C
3,247 ÷ 45 = 72 R7
Check: 72 × 45 = 3,240; 3,240 + 7 = 3,247
Incorrect Answers:
A. The remainder was not included in the answer.
B. In the first subtraction step, regrouping was done incorrectly.
D. 45 divides into 324 seven times, not six.

22. Correct Answer: A
6,981 ÷ 287 = 24 R93
Check: 24 × 287 = 6,888; 6,888 + 93 = 6,981
Incorrect Answers:
B. In the second subtraction step, regrouping was done incorrectly.
C. In the second subtraction step, regrouping was done incorrectly.
D. The remainder was not included in the answer.

23. Correct Answer: B
9,390 ÷ 104 = 90 R30
Check: 90 × 104 = 9,360; 9,360 + 30 = 9,390
Incorrect Answers:
A. The 3 from the first subtraction step was brought up to the answer and no further steps were completed. The 0 from the dividend should have been brought down and written next to the 3, and then 30 should have been divided by 104.
C. The remainder was not included in the answer.
D. 30 cannot be divided by 104; a 0 should have been written in the ones place in the quotient.

Explanations for Test A Answers *(cont.)*

24. Correct Answer: D
There are 31 days in the month of May:
7,719 books ÷ 31 days = 249 books.
Incorrect Answers:
A. 7,719 was divided by 30 days instead of 31 days.
B. *Days* is the wrong label.
C. In the third division step, 31 can go into 279 9 times, not just 8 times.

Adding, Subtracting, Multiplying, and Dividing Decimals (page 16)

25. Correct Answer: B
Align the decimal points before adding:
14.57 + 79.668 = 94.238.
Incorrect Answers:
A. The decimal points were not aligned before adding.
C. The one from the tenths place was not added to the ones place.
D. The decimal point is in the wrong place.

26. Correct Answer: D
Align the decimal points before subtracting:
51.6<u>00</u> – 28.379 = 23.221.
Incorrect Answers:
A. The decimal point is in the wrong place.
B. When regrouping to subtract in the thousandths and hundredths places, the original numbers in the hundredths and tenths places were not reduced by one.
C. The numbers were added instead of subtracted.

27. Correct Answer: A
Align the factors on the right; place the decimal point in the product after multiplying: 8.498 × 6.2 = 52.6876.
Incorrect Answers:
B. The decimal point is in the wrong place.
C. The decimal point is in the wrong place.
D. When multiplying 8.498 by 6 ones, a *0* placeholder was not used in the partial product.

28. Correct Answer: C
Move the decimal point in the divisor until it becomes a whole number; move the decimal point in the dividend the same number of places, and divide:
197.4 ÷ 1.2 = 1,974 ÷ 12 = 164.5.
Incorrect Answers:
A. The decimal point is in the wrong place.
B. All steps of the problem were not completed; division should have continued until the remainder was zero.
D. The decimal point is in the wrong place.

Greatest Common Factor of Two Whole Numbers (page 17)

29. Correct Answer: D
Factors of 12: 1, 2, 3, 4, <u>*6*</u>, 12
Factors of 30: 1, 2, 3, 5, <u>*6*</u>, 10, 15, 30
GCF = 6
Incorrect Answers:
A. 3 is not the *greatest* common factor.
B. 2 is not the *greatest* common factor.
C. 10 is a factor of 30 but is not a factor of 12.

30. Correct Answer: B
Factors of 18: 1, 2, 3, 6, 9, <u>*18*</u>
Factors of 36: 1, 2, 3, 4, 6, 9, 12, <u>*18*</u>, 36
GCF = 18
Incorrect Answers:
A. 9 is not the *greatest* common factor.
C. 6 is not the *greatest* common factor.
D. 3 is not the *greatest* common factor.

31. Correct Answer: C
Factors of 16: 1, 2, 4, <u>*8*</u>, 16
Factors of 24: 1, 2, 3, 4, 6, <u>*8*</u>, 12, 24
GCF = 8
Incorrect Answers:
A. Factors of 4: 1, 2, <u>*4*</u>
Factors of 32: 1, 2, <u>*4*</u>, 8, 16, 32
GCF = 4
B. Factors of 18: 1, 2, 3, 6, <u>*9*</u>, 18
Factors of 27: 1, 3, <u>*9*</u>, 27
GCF = 9
D. Factors of 35: 1, <u>*5*</u>, 7, 35
Factors of 40: 1, 2, 4, <u>*5*</u>, 8, 10, 20, 40
GCF = 5

32. Correct Answer: B
Factors of 21: 1, 3, <u>*7*</u>, 21
Factors of 70: 1, 2, 5, <u>*7*</u>, 10, 14, 35, 70
GCF = 7
Incorrect Answers:
A. Factors of 22: 1, 2, 11, <u>*22*</u>
Factors of 44: 1, 2, 4, 11, <u>*22*</u>, 44
GCF = 22, not 11
C. Factors of 15: 1, 3, 5, <u>*15*</u>
Factors of 45: 1, 3, 5, 9, <u>*15*</u>, 45
GCF = 15, not 5
D. Factors of 24: 1, 2, 3, 4, 6, 8, <u>*12*</u>, 24
Factors of 36: 1, 2, 3, 4, 6, 9, <u>*12*</u>, 18, 36
GCF = 12, not 6

Least Common Multiple of Two Whole Numbers (page 18)

33. Correct Answer: C
Multiples of 4: 4, 8, 12, 16, <u>*20*</u>, 24, 28, 32, ...
Multiples of 5: 5, 10, 15, <u>*20*</u>, 25, 30, 35, 40,...
LCM = 20
Incorrect Answers:
A. 40 is not the *least* common multiple.
B. 15 is a multiple of 5 but is not a multiple of 4.
D. 32 is a multiple of 4 but is not a multiple of 5.

34. Correct Answer: A
Multiples of 8: 8, 16, <u>*24*</u>, 32, 40, 48, 56, ...
Multiples of 12: 12, <u>*24*</u>, 36, 48, 60, 72, ...
LCM = 24
Incorrect Answers:
B. 96 is not the *least* common multiple.
C. 72 is not the *least* common multiple.
D. 48 is not the *least* common multiple.

Explanations for Test A Answers *(cont.)*

35. **Correct Answer: C**
Multiples of 8: 8, 16, 24, 32, *40*, 48, ...
Multiples of 10: 10, 20, 30, *40*, 50, ...
LCM = 40
Incorrect Answers:
A. Multiples of 5: 5, *10*, 15, 20, ...
Multiples of 10: *10*, 20, 30, 40, ...
LCM = 10, not 20
B. Multiples of 3: 3, 6, 9, 12, 15, 18, *21*, 24, 27, 30, 33, 36, 39, 42, ...
Multiples of 7: 7, 14, *21*, 28, 35, 42, 49, 56, ...
LCM = 21, not 42
D. Multiples of 4: 4, 8, 12, 16, 20, 24, 28, 32, *36*, 40, 44, 48, 52, 56, 60, 64, 68, 72, ...
Multiples of 9: 9, 18, 27, *36*, 45, 54, 63, 72, 81, 90, 99, ...
LCM = 36, not 72

36. **Correct Answer: B**
Multiples of 3: 3, 6, *9*, 12, 15, ...
Multiples of 9: *9*, 18, 27, 36, 45, ...
LCM = 9
Incorrect Answers:
A. 18 is the LCM for 3 and 18.
C. 18 is the LCM for 9 and 18.
D. 12 is the LCM for 3 and 12.

Distributive Property (page 19)

37. **Correct Answer: B**
24 + 8 = *32* and 8(3 + 1) = 8(3) + 8(1) = 24 + 8 = 32
Incorrect Answers:
A. 3(8 + 2) = 3(8) + 3(2) = 24 + 6 = 30; 30 ≠ 32
C. (4 × 6) × (4 × 2) = 24 × 8 = 192; 192 ≠ 32
D. (4 × 6) − (4 + 8) = 24 − 12 = 12; 12 ≠ 32

38. **Correct Answer: D**
15 + 10 = *25* and (5 × 3) + (5 × 2) = 15 + 10 = 25
Incorrect Answers:
A. 5(3 × 2) = 5(6) = 30; 30 ≠ 25
B. (5 × 5) + (5 × 2) = 25 + 10 = 35; 35 ≠ 25
C. 3(5 + 2) = 3(5) + 3(2) = 15 + 6 = 21; 21 ≠ 25

39. **Correct Answer: A**
36 + 12 = *48* and *12*(3 + 1) = 12(3) + 12(1) = 36 + 12 = *48*
Incorrect Answers:
B. *4*(3 + 1) = 4(3) + 4(1) = 12 + 4 = 16; 16 ≠ 48
C. *9*(3 + 1) = 9(3) + 9(1) = 27 + 9 = 36; 36 ≠ 48
D. *3*(3 + 1) = 3(3) + 3(1) = 9 + 3 = 12; 12 ≠ 48

40. **Correct Answer: B**
3(9 + 4) = 3(9) + 3(4) = 27 + 12 = *39* and (3 × 9) + (3 × 4) = 27 + 12 = *39*
Incorrect Answers:
A. 12 + 7 = 19; 19 ≠ 39
C. (3 × 9) × (3 × 4) = 27 × 12 = 324; 324 ≠ 39
D. 27 + 7 = 34; 34 ≠ 39

Positive and Negative Numbers (page 20)

41. **Correct Answer: C**
Sudhakar gained 25 points on day 2; a *gain* is represented by a positive integer.
Incorrect Answers:
A. *-25* represents a *loss* of 25 points (day 3).
B. *35* represents a *gain* of 35 points (day 5).
D. *-20* represents a *loss* of 20 points (day 4).

42. **Correct Answer: D**
Sudhakar lost 20 points on day 4; a *loss* is represented by a negative integer.
Incorrect Answers:
A. On day 1, Sudhakar's score was a gain of 20.
B. On day 2, Sudhakar's score was a gain of 25.
C. On day 3, Sudhakar's score was a loss of 25.

43. **Correct Answer: A**
-35 is the lowest score; on the number line, -35 is the furthest away from zero.
Incorrect Answers:
B. -20 is closer to zero than -35, so it is a higher score than -35.
C. 20 is a positive number, so it is a higher score than -35.
D. -25 is closer to zero than -35, so it is a higher score than -35.

44. **Correct Answer: B**
-25 is the opposite of 25.
Incorrect Answers:
A. 25 is not the opposite of 25; it is equal to 25.
C. -35 is a negative integer, but it is not the opposite of 25; it is the opposite integer of 35.
D. 50 cannot be the opposite of 25; it is a positive integer.

Numbers and Their Opposites (page 21)

45. **Correct Answer: B**
The opposite of a negative integer is a positive integer, so the opposite of -3 is 3 (*E*).
Incorrect Answers:
A. *B* = -5
C. *D* = 1
D. *F* = 4

46. **Correct Answer: D**
The opposite of a positive integer is a negative integer, so the opposite of 8 is -8 *(A)*.
Incorrect Answers:
A. *H* = 9
B. *G* = 6
C. *C* = -2

47. **Correct Answer: C**
The opposite of the opposite is the number itself: -(-4) = 4.
Incorrect Answers:
A. -4 = -4; it does not equal -(-4).
B. -(4) = -4; it does not equal -(-4).
D. -(-5) = 5; it does not equal -(-4).

48. **Correct Answer: A**
-10 is the opposite of 10; they are equidistant from 0 on the number line.
Incorrect Answers:
B. $\frac{10}{1}$ = 10
C. $\frac{1}{10}$ and 10 are not equidistant from 0 on the number line.
D. *None of the above* is incorrect because the opposite of 10 is -10 (*A*).

Explanations for Test A Answers *(cont.)*

Ordered Pairs on a Coordinate Plane (page 22)

49. Correct Answer: D

G is located three to the left of zero on the *x*-axis and four below zero on the *y*-axis.

Incorrect Answers:

A. $C = (2,-7)$

B. $F = (-1,4)$

C. $A = (-4,3)$

50. Correct Answer: C

B is located five to the left of zero on the *x*-axis and eight above zero on the *y*-axis.

Incorrect Answers:

A. $H = (8,-5)$.

B. $D = (-6,-5)$

D. $E = (3,0)$

51. Correct Answer: A

F is located one space to the left of zero on the *x*-axis and four spaces above zero on the *y*-axis: (-1,4).

Incorrect Answers:

B. (2,-7) is *C*.

C. (3,0) is *E*.

D. (-6,-5) is *D*.

52. Correct Answer: B

A is located four spaces to the left of zero on the *x*-axis and three spaces above zero on the *y*-axis: (-4,3).

Incorrect Answers:

A. (8,-5) is *H*.

C. (-3,-4) is *G*.

D. (-5,8) is *B*.

Identifying Rational Numbers on a Number Line (page 23)

53. Correct Answer: B

C is located at -1.91.

Incorrect Answers:

A. *J* is located at 2.6.

C. *A* is located at 2.125.

D. *F* is located at 0.6.

54. Correct Answer: C

H is located at 1.5.

Incorrect Answers:

A. *D* is located at -1.5.

B. *I* is located at 2.125.

D. *F* is located at 0.6.

55. Correct Answer: D

A is located at -2.6.

Incorrect Answers:

A. *J* is located at 2.6.

B. *I* is located at $\frac{17}{8}$ (2.125).

C. *B* is located at $-\frac{9}{4}$ (2.25).

56. Correct Answer: B

G is located at 0.67.

Incorrect Answers:

A. *B* is located at $-\frac{9}{4}$ (-2.25).

C. *F* is located at $\frac{3}{5}$ (0.6).

D. *E* is located at -0.7.

Ordering Rational Numbers (page 24)

57. Correct Answer: D

$-\frac{12}{5}$ (-2.4), -1.4, $-\frac{2}{3}$ (-0.67), -0.33 is in order from least to greatest.

Incorrect Answers:

A. -1.4 is greater than $-\frac{12}{5}$, and -0.33 is greater than $-\frac{2}{3}$.

B. -0.33, $-\frac{2}{3}$, -1.4, $-\frac{12}{5}$ is in order from greatest to least.

C. -0.33 is greater than $-\frac{2}{3}$.

58. Correct Answer: B

$\frac{11}{8}$ (1.375), 1.15, -3.12, $-4\frac{1}{8}$ (-4.125) is in order from greatest to least.

Incorrect Answers:

A. $-4\frac{1}{8}$, –3.12, 1.15, $\frac{11}{8}$ is in order from least to greatest.

C. $\frac{11}{8}$ and 1.15 are reversed.

D. $-4\frac{1}{8}$ and -3.12 are reversed.

59. Correct Answer: A

$1\frac{3}{4}$ (1.75), $\frac{5}{8}$ (0.625), 0.4, $-5\frac{3}{7}$ (5.429) is in order from greatest to least.

Incorrect Answers:

B. $-5\frac{3}{7}$ is the least number, not the greatest.

C. $-5\frac{3}{7}$ and 0.4 are reversed.

D. 0.4 and $1\frac{3}{4}$ are switched.

60. Correct Answer: C

$-3\frac{3}{4}$ (-3.75), -3.62, $\frac{7}{2}$ (3.5), 3.81 is in order from least to greatest.

Incorrect Answers:

A. $\frac{7}{2}$ and -3.62 are reversed.

B. 3.81, $\frac{7}{2}$, -3.62, $-3\frac{3}{4}$ is in order from greatest to least.

D. -3.62 and $-3\frac{3}{4}$ are reversed.

Absolute Value of Rational Numbers (page 25)

61. Correct Answer: A

B is five tic marks to the right of zero on the number line, so the integer naming *B* is 5. The absolute value (distance from zero) of *5* is *5*.

Incorrect Answers:

B. *5* and *-5* represent the integer 5 and its opposite; absolute value cannot be negative.

C. *-5* and *5* both represent the integer five tic marks to the *left* of zero and its absolute value.

D. *-5* and *-5* both represent the integer five tic marks to the *left* of zero.

62. Correct Answer: C

H is three tic marks to the left of zero on the number line, so the integer naming *H* is -3. The absolute value (distance from zero) of *-3* is *3*.

Incorrect Answers:

A. *3* and *3* represent the integer three tic marks to the *right* of zero.

B. *-3* and *-3* both represent the integer naming *H*.

D. *3* and *-3* represent the integer three tic marks to the *right* of zero and its opposite.

63. Correct Answer: D

282 feet below sea level is a negative integer: -282. The absolute value (distance from zero) of the integer is 282.

Incorrect Answers:

A. *-282* and *-282* both represent the elevation of Death Valley.

B. *282* and *282* both represent the absolute value of the elevation of Death Valley.

C. *282* and *-282* shows the elevation of Death Valley and its absolute value reversed.

Explanations for Test A Answers *(cont.)*

64. Correct Answer: C
Sunday was the warmest day at -7°. -7 is closer to 0 than -12 is, so -7° is warmer than -12°.
Incorrect Answers:
A. On Friday the temperature was -12°. -12 is further from 0 than -7 on the number line, so -12° is colder than -7°.
B. On Saturday the temperature was -12°. -12 is further from 0 than -7 on the number line, so -12° is colder than -7°.
D. On Friday and Saturday the temperature was -12°. -12 is further from 0 than -7 on the number line, so -12° is colder than -7°.

Expressions with Whole-number Exponents (page 26)

65. Correct Answer: B
The base (8) tells which number to use as a factor, and the exponent (4) tells how many times the base is used as a factor.
$8^4 = 8 \times 8 \times 8 \times 8$
Incorrect Answers:
A. The exponent (4) was incorrectly used as the base, and the base (8) was incorrectly used as the exponent.
C. The base (8) was multiplied by the exponent (4).
D. *B* is correct, so *none of the above* is incorrect.

66. Correct Answer: D
$8^4 = 8 \times 8 \times 8 \times 8 = 4{,}096$
Incorrect Answers:
A. The base (8) was multiplied by the exponent (4).
B. The base (8) and the exponent (4) were added.
C. The base (8) was divided by the exponent (4).

67. Correct Answer: B
The base (6) tells which number to use as a factor, and the exponent (3) tells how many times the base is used as a factor.
$6^3 = 6 \times 6 \times 6$
Incorrect Answers:
A. The base (6) was multiplied by the exponent (3).
C. The exponent (3) was incorrectly used as the base, and the base (6) was incorrectly used as the exponent.
D. *B* is correct, so *none of the above* is incorrect.

68. Correct Answer: C
$6^3 = 6 \times 6 \times 6 = 216$
Incorrect Answers:
A. The exponent (3) was incorrectly used as the base and the base (6) was incorrectly used as the exponent, so 3 was multiplied repeatedly.
B. The base (6) and the exponent (3) were divided.
D. The base (6) was multiplied by the exponent (3).

Variable Expressions (page 27)

69. Correct Answer: C
Product indicates multiplication.
Incorrect Answers:
A. $n + 3$ is a *sum*.
B. $n - 3$ is a *difference*.
D. $n \div 3$ is a *quotient*.

70. Correct Answer: A
Less than indicates subtraction (find the *difference*). *Than* indicates that the order of the terms in the algebraic expression must be reversed from the order in which the terms are written in the word expression.
Incorrect Answers:
B. $8 + b$ represents *a number b more than 8.*
C. $8 - b$ represents *a number b less than 8.*
D. $8 \div b$ represents *8 divided by a number b.*

71. Correct Answer: D
Divided by indicates division.
Incorrect Answers:
A. $f \div 36$ represents *a number f divided by 36.*
B. $36f$ represents *36 times a number f.*
C. $36 + f$ represents *a number f more than 36.*

72. Correct Answer: B
Less than indicates subtraction (find the *difference*). *Than* indicates that the order of the terms in the algebraic expression must be reversed from the order in which the terms are written in the word expression: *2 less than 5 times a number t* is 2 less than $5t$.
Incorrect Answers:
A. $2 - 5t$ represents *5 times a number t less than 2.*
C. The expression was interpreted incorrectly; 2 was subtracted from 5 to get 3, and 3 was multiplied *times a number t.*
D. The expression was interpreted incorrectly; 2 is being subtracted from 5 instead of being subtracted from *5 times a number t.*

Evaluating Expressions (page 28)

73. Correct Answer: C
Replace the variable *b* with 6: $6^2 - 4(4) + 6 \div 2$. Follow order of operations. *EXPONENTS:* $36 - 4(4) + 6 \div 2$. *MULTIPLY/DIVIDE:* $36 - 16 + 3$. *ADD/SUBTRACT:* $20 + 3 = 23$.
Incorrect Answers:
A. 6^2 was calculated as $6 \times 2 = 12$ instead of $6 \times 6 = 36$.
B. The order of operations was not followed; the expression was simplified from left to right.
D. *C* is correct, so *none of the above* is incorrect.

74. Correct Answer: A
Replace the variable *x* with 5: $5^3 - 5(5) + 2(5)$. Follow order of operations. *EXPONENTS:* $125 - 5(5) + 2(5)$. *MULTIPLY/DIVIDE:* $125 - 25 + 10$. *ADD/SUBTRACT:* $100 + 10 = 110$.
Incorrect Answers:
B. 5^3 was calculated as $5 \times 3 = 15$ instead of $5 \times 5 \times 5 = 125$.
C. The order of operations was not followed; the expression was simplified from left to right.
D. *A* is correct, so *none of the above* is incorrect.

75. Correct Answer: D
Replace the variable *g* with 2 since Amit is bowling *2* games: $3(2) + 1$. Multiply 3×2 to find the cost of 2 games (₹6). Add the cost of the shoe rental to the cost of the 2 games to find the total cost: ₹6 + ₹1 = ₹7.
Incorrect Answers:
A. The cost of each game (₹3) was added to the one time fee of (₹1) before multiplying by the total number of games (2).
B. ₹4 represents the cost of *one* game of bowling and the shoe rental fee.
C. ₹5 indicates that each game of bowling cost ₹1 and the shoe rental fee was ₹3.

Explanations for Test A Answers *(cont.)*

76. Correct Answer: B
Replace the variable *h* with 6 since Ferheena babysat for 6 hours: 9(6) + 5. Multiply 6 × ₹9 to determine the charge for 6 hours of babysitting (₹54). Add the charge for preparing lunch to the charge for babysitting to find the total amount that Ferheena will charge for babysitting: ₹54 + ₹5 = ₹59.
Incorrect Answers:
- **A.** ₹14 represents the charge for *one* hour of babysitting plus a ₹5 charge for preparing lunch.
- **C.** The charge for one hour of babysitting was added to the one-time charge for preparing lunch before multiplying by the number of hours she babysat.
- **D.** The charge for preparing lunch was not included in the equation.

Equivalent Expressions (page 29)

77. Correct Answer: B
Apply the distributive property by multiplying the term outside the parentheses by the terms inside the parentheses:
7 times x plus 7 times 9 = $7x + 63$.
Incorrect Answers:
- **A.** x was not multiplied by 7.
- **C.** 7 and 9 were added instead of multiplied.
- **D.** 9 was not multiplied by 7.

78. Correct Answer: A
Use the distributive property in reverse to factor the expression. The greatest common factor of $36x$ and $18y$ is 18, so divide both terms by 18 to get $18(2x + y)$. Check by using the distributive property.
Incorrect Answers:
- **B.** The terms were incorrectly added together (unlike terms cannot be added).
- **C.** 2 was used as the common factor of $36x$ and $18y$ and was written outside of the parentheses, but the original terms were not divided by 2.
- **D.** $18y$ was not divided by the greatest common factor (18).

79. Correct Answer: C
Apply the distributive property by multiplying the term outside the parentheses by the terms inside the parentheses:
5 times y and 5 times -5 = $5y - 25$.
Incorrect Answers:
- **A.** y was not multiplied by 5.
- **B.** -5 was not multiplied by 5.
- **D.** *C* is correct, so *none of the above* is incorrect.

80. Correct Answer: B
Use the distributive property in reverse to factor the expression. The greatest common factor of 24 and $48y$ is 24, so divide both factors by 24 to get $24(1 + 2y)$. Check by using the distributive property.
Incorrect Answers:
- **A.** 24 was added to the coefficient of the term $48y$.
- **C.** The term $2y$ was incorrectly written; the variable y should be omitted because there is no y in the first term of the original expression.
- **D.** 24 was not divided by the greatest common factor (24).

One-variable Equations and Inequalities (page 30)

81. Correct Answer: D
$9 + 3(4) = 9 + 12 = 21$
Incorrect Answers:
- **A.** $9 + 3(7) = 9 + 21 = 30;\ 30 \neq 21$
- **B.** $9 + 3(12) = 9 + 36 = 45;\ 45 \neq 21$
- **C.** $9 + 3(9) = 9 + 27 = 36;\ 36 \neq 21$

82. Correct Answer: B
$32 - 8 = 24$ and $14 + 7 = 21;\ 24 > 21$
Incorrect Answers:
- **A.** $32 - 12 = 20$ and $14 + 7 = 21;\ 20 < 21$
- **C.** $32 - 11 = 21$ and $14 + 7 = 21;\ 21 = 21$
- **D.** $32 - 21 = 11$ and $14 + 7 = 21;\ 11 < 21$

83. Correct Answer: C
$54 \div 6 = 9$
Incorrect Answers:
- **A.** $4 + 2n = 4 + 2(6) = 4 + 12 = 16.\ 16 \neq 12$. The 4 from the original expression was not included in the calculations.
- **B.** $3 \times (3n) = 3 \times (3 \times 6) = 3 \times 18 = 54;\ 54 \neq 36$.
- **D.** $19 - n + 3 = 19 - 6 + 3 = 16.\ 16 \neq 13$. The +3 from the original expression was not included in the calculations.

84. Correct Answer: C
$7 \times n = 7 \times 5 = 35$
Incorrect Answers:
- **A.** $3 + 5 = 8$ and $8 = 8$ (8 is not less than 8).
- **B.** $25 - 5 = 20;\ 20 \neq 30$
- **D.** $40 \div (2 \times 5) = 40 \div 10 = 4;\ 4 \neq 8$

Area (page 31)

85. Correct Answer: A
The area of the parallelogram is the area of the rectangle:
$A = bh = 12(4) = 48$ in.^{2}
Incorrect Answers:
- **B.** Only half of the length of the base of the parallelogram was used to solve, and the label is incorrect.
- **C.** The label is incorrect; area is labeled in square units.
- **D.** Only half of the length of the base of the parallelogram was used to solve.

86. Correct Answer: D
$A = \frac{1}{2}bh = \frac{1}{2}(10)(16) = 5(16) = 80$ cm^2
Incorrect Answers:
- **A.** The label is incorrect; area is labeled in square units.
- **B.** The base was not multiplied by $\frac{1}{2}$.
- **C.** The base was not multiplied by $\frac{1}{2}$, and the label is incorrect.

87. Correct Answer: C
$A = \frac{1}{2}bh = \frac{1}{2}(12)(9) = 6(9) = 54$ cm^2
Incorrect Answers:
- **A.** The base was not multiplied by $\frac{1}{2}$.
- **B.** The label is incorrect; area is labeled in square units.
- **D.** The base was not multiplied by $\frac{1}{2}$, and the label is incorrect.

Explanations for Test A Answers *(cont.)*

88. Correct Answer: D
$A = \frac{1}{2}h(b_1 + b_2) = \frac{1}{2}(8)(10 + 12) = \frac{1}{2}(8)(22) = 4(22) = 88 \text{ in.}^2$
Incorrect Answers:
A. The label is incorrect; area is labeled in square units.
B. $Base_1$ (10 in.) and $base_2$ (12 in.) were added together and multiplied by $\frac{1}{2}$; the height was not included in the calculations.
C. $Base_1$ (10 in.) and $base_2$ (12 in.) were added together and multiplied by $\frac{1}{2}$; the height was not included in the calculations. The label is incorrect.

Volume of Rectangular Prisms with Fractional Sides (page 32)

89. Correct Answer: B
$V = l \times w \times h = 5\frac{1}{2} \times 2 \times 3 = \frac{11}{2} \times 2 \times 3 = 11 \times 3 = 33 \text{ in}^3$.
Incorrect Answers:
A. The label is incorrect; volume is labeled in cubic units.
C. A multiplication error occurred: $\frac{11}{2} \times 2 \neq 22$.
D. The wrong operation (addition) was used.

90. Correct Answer: A
$V = l \times w \times h = 4\frac{1}{2} \times 5 \times 4 = \frac{9}{2} \times 5 \times 4 = 90 \text{ cm}^3$
Incorrect Answers:
B. A multiplication error occurred: $\frac{9}{2} \times 4 \neq 36$.
C. The wrong operation (addition) was used.
D. The label is incorrect; volume is labeled in cubic units.

91. Correct Answer: D
$V = l \times w \times h = 2\frac{1}{4} \times 3 \times 4 = \frac{9}{4} \times 3 \times 4 = 27 \text{ ft}^3$.
Incorrect Answers:
A. The wrong operation (addition) was used.
B. The label is incorrect; volume is labeled in cubic units.
C. A multiplication error occurred: $\frac{9}{4} \times 4 \neq 36$.

92. Correct Answer: D
$V = l \times w \times h = 7 \times 3\frac{1}{3} \times 3 = 7 \times \frac{10}{3} \times 3 = \frac{70}{3} \times 3 = 70 \text{ yd}^3$.
Incorrect Answers:
A. The label is incorrect; volume is labeled in cubic units.
B. A multiplication error occurred: $\frac{70}{3} \times 3 \neq 210$.
C. The wrong operation (addition) was used.

Dot Plots (page 33)

93. Correct Answer: B
0 + 2 + 3 + 6 + 9 + 10 + 8 + 7 + 6 + 5 + 3 + 1 = 60 days
Incorrect Answers:
A. 54 days does not include the 6 rainy days in April or September.
C. 55 days does not include the 5 rainy days in October.
D. 51 days does not include the 9 rainy days in May.

94. Correct Answer: C
mean = (0 + 2 + 3 + 6 + 9 + 10 + 8 + 7 + 6 + 5 + 3 + 1) ÷ 12 = 60 ÷ 12 = 5
Incorrect Answers:
A. 12 is the number of months.
B. 10 days is the greatest number of rainy days in one month (June).
D. 5.5 days is the median of the data.

95. Correct Answer: A
Order the values from least to greatest:
0, 1, 2, 3, 3, 5, 6, 6, 7, 8, 9, 10. Since there is an even number of data values, the median is the mean of the middle two numbers: median = (5 + 6) ÷ 2 = 11 ÷ 2 = 5.5 days.
Incorrect Answers:
B. 5 is the mean.
C. 6 is one of the numbers in the middle of the data, but it is not the middle value.
D. 0 is the least number of rainy days in the year, not the median.

96. Correct Answer: D
The values on the dot plot all lie relatively close together—no one data value lies far away from the other values—so there is no outlier.
Incorrect Answers:
A. 0 is the least value on the plot, but it does not lie far away from the next value (2).
B. 10 is the greatest value on the plot. It does not lie far away from its neighboring values (9 and 8).
C. 1 is the least value on the plot, but it does not lie far away from the next value (3).

Histograms and Box Plots (page 34)

97. Correct Answer: C
The number of bags sold with the greatest frequency is 50–69 bags: 50–59 = frequency of 9 and 60–69 = frequency of 10. The cluster occurs between 50–69 bags.
Incorrect Answers:
A. 40–49 bags only has a frequency of 2; a cluster of data does not occur here.
B. 50–59 is only part of the cluster; 60–69 occurs with the highest frequency on the plot and should also be part of the cluster.
D. 70–79 bags only has a frequency of 3; a cluster of data does not occur here.

98. Correct Answer: A
4, 4, 5, 8, 8, 10, 10: 8 is the number in the middle of the list, so it is the median.
Incorrect Answers:
B. 10 is the greatest number in the data.
C. 5 is not the number in the middle of the list.
D. 4 is the least number in the data.

99. Correct Answer: D
Calculate the mean:
mean = (4 + 4 + 5 + 8 + 8 + 10 + 10) ÷ 7 = 49 ÷ 7 = 7.
Then calculate the difference between the mean and each data value: 7 – 4 = *3*; 7 – 4 = *3*; 7 – 5 = *2*; 8 – 7 = *1*; 8 – 7 = *1*; 10 – 7 = *3*; 10 – 7 = *3*.
Finally, calculate the mean of the differences: mean absolute deviation = (3 + 3 + 2 + 1 + 1 + 3 + 3) ÷ 7 = 16 ÷ 7 = 2.28.
Incorrect Answers:
A. 49 is the total of the data values.
B. 16 is the total of the differences.
C. 7 is the mean, not the mean absolute deviation.

100. Correct Answer: B
10 (3rd quartile) – 4 (1st quartile) = 6
Incorrect Answers:
A. 10 is the 3rd quartile.
C. 4 is the 1st quartile.
D. 49 is the total of the data values.

Explanations for Test B Answers

Ratios (page 35)

1. Correct Answer: D

There are 2 triangles and 3 squares; the ratio of triangles to squares can be written 2:3, $\frac{2}{3}$, or 2 to 3.

Incorrect Answers:

- **A.** The numbers were written in the wrong order; 3:2, $\frac{3}{2}$, and 3 to 2 represent the ratio of squares to triangles.
- **B.** 2:5, $\frac{2}{5}$, and 2 to 5 represent the ratio of triangles to circles.
- **C.** 2:10, $\frac{2}{10}$, and 2 to 10 represent the ratio of triangles to total number of shapes.

2. Correct Answer: C

There are 5 circles and 3 squares; the ratio of circles to squares can be written 5:3, $\frac{5}{3}$, or 5 to 3.

Incorrect Answers:

- **A.** The numbers were written in the wrong order; 3:5, $\frac{3}{5}$, and 3 to 5 represent the ratio of squares to circles.
- **B.** 5:2, $\frac{5}{2}$, and 5 to 2 represent the ratio of circles to triangles.
- **D.** 5:10, $\frac{5}{10}$, and 5 to 10 represent the ratio of circles to the total number of shapes.

3. Correct Answer: B

Compare the number of votes Deepak received (98) to the number of votes Naveen received (123) to find the ratio of votes for Deepak to the number of votes for Naveen.

Incorrect Answers:

- **A.** 123:98 represents the ratio of votes for Naveen to the number of votes for Deepak.
- **C.** 221:98 represents the ratio of total number of votes to the number of votes for Deepak.
- **D.** 123:221 represents the ratio of votes for Naveen to the total number of votes.

4. Correct Answer: C

12 peanut butter + 24 chocolate chip + 6 oatmeal raisin = 42 cookies baked. Compare the number of peanut butter cookies (12) to the total number of cookies (42) to find the ratio.

Incorrect Answers:

- **A.** The numbers were written in the wrong order; 42:12 represents the ratio of total number of cookies to the number of peanut butter cookies.
- **B.** 12:30 represents the number of peanut butter cookies to the number of chocolate chip and oatmeal raisin cookies.
- **D.** 30:12 represents the number of chocolate chip and oatmeal raisin cookies to the number of peanut butter cookies.

Ratio Relationships (page 36)

5. Correct Answer: C

Start with the ratio 2:5. Rewrite the ratio as a fraction: $\frac{2}{5}$. Since $2 \times 4 = 8$, multiply the numerator and denominator of the fraction by 4 to complete the ratio table: $\frac{2}{5} = \frac{8}{20}$.

Incorrect Answers:

- **A.** 4 was subtracted from the next number in the column (25).
- **B.** 4 was added to the previous number in the column (15).
- **D.** Since $6 + 2 = 8$ (in the first column), 2 was added to 15 in the second column to get 17.

6. Correct Answer: B

Start with the ratio 6:4. Rewrite the ratio as a fraction: $\frac{6}{4}$. Since $6 \times 3 = 18$, multiply the numerator and denominator of the fraction by 3 to complete the ratio table: $\frac{6}{4} = \frac{18}{12}$.

Incorrect Answers:

- **A.** Since $12 + 6 = 18$ (in the first column), 6 was added to 8 in the second column to get 14.
- **C.** 3 was added to the previous number in the column (8).
- **D.** 3 was subtracted from the next number in the column (16).

7. Correct Answer: D

The ratio of miles to gallons is $\frac{32}{2}$. To find an equivalent fraction with a numerator of 160 (160 miles to Naveen's friend's cabin), multiply the numerator and denominator by 5: $\frac{32}{2} = \frac{160}{10}$.

Incorrect Answers:

- **A.** 6 gallons of petrol was calculated by adding 1 gallon of petrol in each row of the table until 160 miles was reached in the left column of the table.
- **B.** 5 was added to 2 instead of being multiplied by 2.
- **C.** 160 is the number of miles driven, not the number of gallons of petrol used.

8. Correct Answer: B

The ratio of shots taken to baskets made is $\frac{10}{7}$. To find an equivalent fraction with a denominator of 35 (35 baskets made), multiply the numerator and denominator by 5: $\frac{10}{7} = \frac{50}{35}$.

Incorrect Answers:

- **A.** 14 times was calculated by adding 1 shot taken in every row (starting with 10 shots taken for 7 baskets made) of the table until 35 baskets made was reached in the right column.
- **C.** The first row of the table was filled in correctly with 10 and 7. Then, since $7 + 28 = 35$ baskets made, 28 was added to 10 shots taken to get 38 shots taken.
- **D.** 5 times was calculated by adding 1 shot taken in every row (starting with 1 shot taken for 7 baskets made) of the table until 35 baskets made was reached in the right column.

Unit Rate Ratios (page 37)

9. Correct Answer: A

Write the number of miles over the number of gallons to find the rate: $\frac{270 \text{ miles}}{15 \text{ gallons}}$. The fraction bar indicates division, so divide the number of miles (270) by the number of gallons (15) to find the unit rate: $\frac{18 \text{ miles}}{1 \text{ gallon}}$. The second number of a unit rate is always 1.

Incorrect Answers:

- **B.** When finding the unit rate, the numerator of the rate (270) was correctly divided by 15, but the denominator was not divided by 15.
- **C.** The values were reversed when writing the rate.
- **D.** *A* is correct, so *none of the above* is incorrect.

10. Correct Answer: C

Write the amount of money over the number of weeks to find the rate: $\frac{₹255}{5 \text{ weeks}}$. The fraction bar indicates division, so divide the amount of money (₹255) by the number of weeks (5) to find the unit rate: $\frac{₹51}{1 \text{ week}}$. The second number of a unit rate is always 1.

Incorrect Answers:

- **A.** A division error occurred when finding the unit rate.
- **B.** When finding the unit rate, the numerator of the rate (₹255) was correctly divided by 5, but the denominator was not divided by 5.
- **D.** *C* is correct, so *none of the above* is incorrect.

Explanations for Test B Answers *(cont.)*

11. Correct Answer: B
Find the unit rate: $\frac{36 \text{ minutes}}{9 \text{ pages}} = \frac{4 \text{ minutes}}{1 \text{ page}}$. Multiply the unit rate $\frac{4 \text{ minutes}}{1 \text{ page}}$ by the number of pages to read (27) to find how long it will take Vicky to read to 27 pages (108 minutes).
Incorrect Answers:
A. The unit rate was not calculated; 36 minutes was multiplied by 27 pages.
C. 4 minutes is the amount of time it takes Vicky to read one page (the unit rate).
D. The unit rate was calculated incorrectly: 27 pages was divided by 9 pages to get 3 as the unit rate. Then 27 pages was multiplied by 3.

12. Correct Answer: C
Find the unit rate: $\frac{144 \text{ pencils}}{12 \text{ boxes}} = \frac{12 \text{ pencils}}{1 \text{ box}}$. Multiply the unit rate $\frac{12 \text{ pencils}}{1 \text{ box}}$ by the number of boxes (16) to find the total number of pencils (192).
Incorrect Answers:
A. The unit rate was not found; 144 pencils was divided by 16.
B. 12 pencils is the unit rate (the number of pencils per box).
D. 12 boxes of pencils was subtracted from 16 boxes of pencils for a difference of 4 boxes. 144 (pencils) was multiplied by the difference (4) for a total of 576 pencils.

Percent (page 38)

13. Correct Answer: D
$35\% = \frac{35}{100}$. *Of* means *multiply:* $\frac{35}{100} \times \frac{900}{1} = \frac{35}{1} \times \frac{9}{1}$ (after cross-cancelling) $= \frac{315}{1} = 315$.
Incorrect Answers:
A. 35% was incorrectly converted to $\frac{100}{35}$ and 900 was incorrectly converted to $\frac{1}{900}$.
B. 35% was incorrectly converted to $\frac{35}{1,000}$.
C. 35% was incorrectly converted to $\frac{35}{10}$.

14. Correct Answer: A
$110\% = \frac{110}{100}$. *Of* means *multiply:* $\frac{110}{100} \times \frac{500}{1} = \frac{110}{1} \times \frac{5}{1}$ (after cross-cancelling) $= \frac{550}{1} = 550$.
Incorrect Answers:
B. 110% was incorrectly converted to $\frac{110}{10}$.
C. 110% was incorrectly converted to $\frac{110}{1,000}$.
D. 110% was incorrectly converted to $\frac{100}{110}$ and 500 was incorrectly converted to $\frac{1}{500}$.

15. Correct Answer: B
Ferheena received 65% *of* the 80 votes. *Of* means *multiply* and $65\% = \frac{65}{100}$: $\frac{65}{100} \times \frac{80}{1} = \frac{65}{5} \times \frac{4}{1}$ (after cross-cancelling) $= \frac{260}{5} = 52$.
Incorrect Answers:
A. 60% was used to solve instead of 65%.
C. An error occurred when reducing $\frac{260}{5}$: $260 \div 5 \neq 50$.
D. 15 is the difference between 80 and 65 (the two numbers included in the problem).

16. Correct Answer: C
Ferheena plans to use 15% of her allowance to purchase a scrapbook. *Of* means *multiply* and $15\% = \frac{15}{100}$:
$\frac{15}{100} \times \frac{200}{1} = \frac{15}{1} \times \frac{2}{1}$ (after cross-cancelling) $= \frac{30}{1} = 30$.
Incorrect Answers:
A. 15% was incorrectly converted to $\frac{15}{1,000}$.
B. 15% was incorrectly converted to $\frac{15}{10}$.
D. A multiplication error occurred: $\frac{15}{100} \times \frac{200}{1} \neq \frac{1,200}{100}$ (a zero placeholder was not used when multiplying 200 by the one in 15).

Dividing Fractions (page 39)

17. Correct Answer: B
Change division to multiplication, and change the divisor to its reciprocal: $\frac{9}{10} \times \frac{5}{3} = \frac{3}{2} \times \frac{1}{1}$ (after cross-cancelling) $= \frac{3}{2} = 1\frac{1}{2}$.
Incorrect Answers:
A. The answer was not simplified.
C. The dividend was changed to its reciprocal instead of the divisor.
D. Division was changed to multiplication, but the divisor was not changed to its reciprocal.

18. Correct Answer: C
Change division to multiplication, and change the divisor to its reciprocal: $\frac{5}{6} \times \frac{8}{3} = \frac{5}{3} \times \frac{4}{3}$ (after cross-cancelling) $= \frac{20}{9} = 2\frac{2}{9}$.
Incorrect Answers:
A. The dividend was changed to its reciprocal instead of the divisor.
B. The answer was not simplified.
D. Division was changed to multiplication, but the divisor was not changed to its reciprocal.

19. Correct Answer: D
Divide $\frac{5}{8}$ gallon by $\frac{2}{16}$ gallon per serving to find how many $\frac{2}{16}$-gallon servings of lemonade Vicky can pour:
$\frac{5}{8} \div \frac{2}{16} = \frac{5}{8} \times \frac{16}{2} = \frac{5}{1} \times \frac{2}{2}$ (after cross-cancelling) $= \frac{10}{2} = 5$.
Incorrect Answers:
A. The divisor and the dividend were reversed: $\frac{2}{16} \div \frac{5}{8}$.
B. Division was changed to multiplication, but the divisor was not changed to its reciprocal.
C. Both the divisor and the dividend were changed to their reciprocals.

20. Correct Answer: C
Divide the $\frac{7}{8}$-metre door by $\frac{1}{4}$-metre boards to find how many boards Nitin will use to build the door: $\frac{7}{8} \div \frac{1}{4} = \frac{7}{8} \times \frac{4}{1} = \frac{7}{2} \times \frac{1}{1}$ (after cross-cancelling) $= \frac{7}{2} = 3\frac{1}{2}$.
Incorrect Answers:
A. The answer was not simplified.
B. The divisor and the dividend were reversed: $\frac{1}{4} \div \frac{7}{8}$.
D. Both the divisor and the dividend were changed to their reciprocals.

Dividing Multi-digit Numbers (page 40)

21. Correct Answer: A
5,102 ÷ 83 = 61 R39
Check: 61 × 83 = 5,063; 5,063 + 39 = 5,102
Incorrect Answers:
B. In the second subtraction step, the digits in the ones column were added instead of subtracted.
C. 83 divides into 510 six times, not five.
D. The remainder was not included in the answer.

22. Correct Answer: D
3,111 ÷ 29 = 107 R8
Check: 107 × 29 = 3,103; 3,103 + 8 = 3,111
Incorrect Answers:
A. In the second division step, 29 cannot divide into 21. A zero should have been placed in the tens place in the quotient.
B. The remainder was not included in the answer.
C. In the third division step, 29 divides into 211 seven times, not six.

Explanations for Test B Answers *(cont.)*

23. Correct Answer: B
8,593 ÷ 216 = 39 R169
Check: 39 × 216 = 8,424; 8,424 + 169 = 8,593
Incorrect Answers:
A. In the second subtraction step the digits in the hundreds column were not subtracted.
C. The remainder was not included in the answer.
D. The quotient and the remainder were reversed.

24. Correct Answer: B
8,198 seats ÷ 264 seats per row = 31 rows, with a remainder of 14 seats.
Incorrect Answers:
A. The label for the remainder is *seats*, not *rows*; there are 14 seats left over that do not make a complete row, not 14 rows.
C. The remainder was not included in the answer.
D. The labels for the quotient and the remainder were reversed.

Adding, Subtracting, Multiplying, and Dividing Decimals (page 41)

25. Correct Answer: A
Align the factors on the right; place the decimal point in the product after multiplying: 4.77 × 5.4 = 25.758
Incorrect Answers:
B. The decimal point is in the wrong place.
C. The decimal point is in the wrong place.
D. A comma was used instead of a decimal point.

26. Correct Answer: B
Align the decimal points before adding: 37.162 + 9.3 = 46.462.
Incorrect Answers:
A. The decimal points were not aligned before adding; the numbers were aligned flush right.
C. The decimal point is in the wrong place.
D. The decimal points were not aligned before adding; the numbers were aligned flush left.

27. Correct Answer: B
Move the decimal point in the divisor until it becomes a whole number; move the decimal point in the dividend the same number of places, and divide: 0.6 ÷ 0.75 = 0.8.
Incorrect Answers:
A. The divisor was divided by the dividend.
C. The decimal point is in the wrong place.
D. The decimal point is in the wrong place.

28. Correct Answer: A
Align the decimal points before subtracting:
15.07 – 4.294 = 10.776.
Incorrect Answers:
B. The numbers were reversed: 15.07 was subtracted from 4.294. Decimals were ignored until placed in answers.
C. The wrong operation (addition) was used.
D. The decimal point is in the wrong place.

Greatest Common Factor of Two Whole Numbers (page 42)

29. Correct Answer: A
Factors of 18: 1, 2, 3, 6, _9_, 18
Factors of 63: 1, 3, 7, _9_, 21, 63
GCF = 9
Incorrect Answers:
B. 6 is a factor of 18, but is not a factor of 63.
C. 3 is not the *greatest* common factor.
D. 7 is a factor of 63 but is not a factor of 18.

30. Correct Answer: C
Factors of 24: 1, 2, 3, 4, _6_, 8, 12, 24
Factors of 42: 1, 2, 3, _6_, 7, 14, 21, 42
GCF = 6
Incorrect Answers:
A. 3 is not the *greatest* common factor.
B. 4 is a factor of 24 but is not a factor of 42.
D. 2 is not the *greatest* common factor.

31. Correct Answer: D
Factors of 45: 1, 3, 5, _9_, 15, 45
Factors of 72: 1, 2, 3, 4, 6, 8, _9_, 12, 18, 24, 36, 72
GCF = 9
Incorrect Answers:
A. Factors of 35: 1, 5, _7_, 35
Factors of 56: 1, 2, 4, _7_, 8,14, 28, 56
GCF = 7
B. Factors of 6: 1, 2, 3, _6_
Factors of 48: 1, 2, 3, 4, _6_, 8, 12, 16, 24, 48
GCF = 6
C. Factors of 10: 1, 2, _5_, 10
Factors of 25: 1, _5_, 25
GCF = 5

32. Correct Answer: C
Factors of 16: 1, 2, _4_, 8, 16
Factors of 20: 1, 2, _4_, 5, 10, 20
GCF = 4
Incorrect Answers:
A. Factors of 14: 1, 2, 7, _14_
Factors of 28: 1, 2, 4, 7, _14_, 28
GCF = 14, not 7
B. Factors of 20: 1, 2, 4, 5, 10, _20_
Factors of 40: 1, 2, 4, 5, 8, 10, _20_, 40
GCF = 20, not 10
D. Factors of 45: 1, 3, 5, _9_, 15, 45
Factors of 54: 1, 2, 3, 6, _9_, 18, 27, 54
GCF = 9, not 3

Least Common Multiple of Two Whole Numbers (page 43)

33. Correct Answer: D
Multiples of 2: 2, 4, _6_, 8, 10, 12, ...
Multiples of 6: _6_, 12, 18, 24, 30, 36, ...
LCM = 6
Incorrect Answers:
A. 18 is not the *least* common multiple.
B. 12 is not the *least* common multiple.
C. 30 is not the *least* common multiple.

Explanations for Test B Answers *(cont.)*

34. Correct Answer: B
Multiples of 3: 3, 6, 9, 12, 15, 18, 21, 24, 27, *30*, ...
Multiples of 10: 10, 20, *30*, 40, 50, 60, 70, 80, 90, 100, ...
LCM = 30
Incorrect Answers:
A. 50 is a multiple of 10 but is not a multiple of 3.
C. 60 is not the *least* common multiple.
D. 20 is a multiple of 10 but is not a multiple of 3.

35. Correct Answer: C
Multiples of 4: 4, 8, *12*, 16, 20, ...
Multiples of 12: *12*, 24, 36, 48, 60, ...
LCM = 12
Incorrect Answers:
A. Multiples of 7: 7, 14, 21, 28, 35, 42, 49, 56, *63*, ...
Multiples of 9: 9, 18, 27, 36, 45, 54, *63*, 72, 81, ...
LCM = 63, not 56
B. Multiples of 3: 3, 6, 9, 12, 15, 18, 21, *24*, 27, 30, 33, 36, 39, 42, 45, 48, ...
Multiples of 8: 8, 16, *24*, 32, 40, 48, 56, 64, 72, ...
LCM = 24, not 48
D. Multiples of 5: 5, 10, 15, 20, 25, *30*, 35, 40, 45, 50, 55, 60, ...
Multiples of 6: 6, 12, 18, 24, *30*, 36, 42, 48, 54, 60, ...
LCM = 30, not 60

36. Correct Answer: A
Multiples of 3: 3, *6*, 9, 12, 15, ...
Multiples of 6: *6*, 12, 18, 24, 30, ...
LCM = 6
Incorrect Answers:
B. Multiples of 3: 3, 6, *9*, 12, ...
Multiples of 9: *9*, 18, 27, 36, ...; LCM = 9
C. Multiples of 12: 12, 24, *36*, ...
Multiples of 18: 18, *36*, 54, ...; LCM = 36
D. Multiples of 6: 6, *12*, 18, 24, ...
Multiples of 12: *12*, 24, 36, 48, ...; LCM = 12

Distributive Property *(page 44)*

37. Correct Answer: D
54 + 18 = *72* and 9(6 + 2) = 9(6) + 9(2) = 54 + 18 = *72*
Incorrect Answers:
A. 6(9 + 2) = 6(9) + 6(2) = 54 + 12 = 66; 66 ≠ 72
B. (9 × 6) × (9 × 2) = 54 × 18 = 972; 972 ≠ 72
C. 9(6 × 2) = 9(12) = 108; 108 ≠ 72

38. Correct Answer: A
42 + 21 = *63* and 7(6 + 3) = 7(6) + 7(3) = 42 + 21 = *63*
Incorrect Answers:
B. (6 × 7) + (6 × 3) = 42 + 18 = 60; 60 ≠ 63
C. 7(6 × 3) = 7(18) = 126; 126 ≠ 63
D. (7 × 6) × (7 × 3) = 42 × 21 = 882; 882 ≠ 63

39. Correct Answer: A
28 + 16 = *44* and 4(7 + *4*) = 4(7) + 4(4) = 28 + 16 = *44*
Incorrect Answers:
B. 4(7 + *8*) = 4(7) + 4(8) = 28 + 32 = 60; 60 ≠ 44
C. 4(7 + *2*) = 4(7) + 4(2) = 28 + 8 = 36; 36 ≠ 44
D. 4(7 + *12*) = 4(7) + 4(12) = 28 + 48 = 76; 76 ≠ 44

40. Correct Answer: B
5(8 + 7) = 5(8) + 5(7) = 40 + 35 = *75* and 40 + 35 = *75*
Incorrect Answers:
A. 40 × 35 = 1,400; 1,400 ≠ 75
C. (5 × 8) – (5 × 7) = 40 – 35 = 5; 5 ≠ 75
D. (5 + 8) × (5 + 7) = 13 × 12 = 156; 156 ≠ 75

Positive and Negative Numbers *(page 45)*

41. Correct Answer: B
122° above zero = 122; 34° below zero = -34
Incorrect Answers:
A. -122 = 122° below zero, not above; 34 = 34° above zero, not below.
C. 34 = 34° above zero, not below.
D. -122 = 122° below zero, not above.

42. Correct Answer: C
Montana's lowest temperature is -45°. On the number line, -45 is the furthest away from the zero on the left.
Incorrect Answers:
A. Delaware had the warmest low temperature.
B. -15° is 30 degrees warmer than Montana's lowest temperature.
D. -25° is 20 degrees warmer than Montana's lowest temperature.

43. Correct Answer: C
Delaware's highest temperature was 112°; the opposite of 112 is -112.
Incorrect Answers:
A. 9 is the opposite of Delaware's lowest temperature, -9°.
B. 112 is the same as 112°, not the opposite.
D. -134 is the opposite of Montana's highest temperature, 134°.

44. Correct Answer: A
101° above zero = 101; 15° below zero = -15
Incorrect Answers:
B. 15 = 15° above zero, not below.
C. -15° is New York's lowest temperature and 101° is the highest temperature; the temperatures were reversed.
D. -101 = 101° below zero, not above.

Numbers and Their Opposites *(page 46)*

45. Correct Answer: C
The opposite of positive integer is a negative integer, so the opposite of 6 is -6 (*B*).
Incorrect Answers:
A. *G* = 5
B. *C* = -3
D. *A* = -7

46. Correct Answer: A
The opposite of a negative integer is a positive integer, so the opposite of -9 is 9 (*H*).
Incorrect Answers:
B. *G* = 5
C. *E* = 2
D. *D* = -1

Explanations for Test B Answers *(cont.)*

47. Correct Answer: D
The opposite of the opposite is the number itself: 7 = -(-7).
Incorrect Answers:
A. -(7) = -7
B. -7 = -7
C. 0 = 0

48. Correct Answer: B
The opposite of the opposite is the number itself: -(-2) = 2.
Incorrect Answers:
A. -2 = -2
C. -(2) = -2
D. 4 = 4

Ordered Pairs on a Coordinate Plane *(page 47)*

49. Correct Answer: B
D is located seven to the left of zero on the *x*-axis and three above zero on the *y*-axis.
Incorrect Answers:
A. *A* = (7,-3)
C. *B* = (-8,-3)
D. *F* = (6,6)

50. Correct Answer: B
E is located six to the right of zero on the *x*-axis and two below zero on the *y*-axis.
Incorrect Answers:
A. *G* = (-6,2)
C. *C* = (4,-4)
D. *H* = (-2,-4)

51. Correct Answer: D
H is located two to the left of zero on the *x*-axis and four below zero on the *y*-axis: (-2,-4).
Incorrect Answers:
A. (-8,-3) is *B*.
B. (1,4) is not labeled on the coordinate plane.
C. (4,-4) is *C*.

52. Correct Answer: A
C is located four to the right of zero on the *x*-axis and four below zero on the *y*-axis: (4,-4).
Incorrect Answers:
B. (-4,4) is not labeled on the coordinate plane.
C. (4,4) is not labeled on the coordinate plane.
D. (-4,-4) is not labeled on the coordinate plane.

Identifying Rational Numbers on a Number Line *(page 48)*

53. Correct Answer: D
$1\frac{2}{5}$ = 1.4 = *H*
Incorrect Answers:
A. *G* is located at $1\frac{1}{4}$ (1.25).
B. *B* is located at $-1\frac{2}{5}$ (-1.4).
C. *C* is located at $-1\frac{1}{4}$ (-1.25).

54. Correct Answer: D
$-\frac{4}{5}$ = -0.8 = *D*
Incorrect Answers:
A. *F* is located at $\frac{4}{5}$ (0.8).
B. *J* is located at $2\frac{3}{4}$ (2.75).
C. *E* is located at -0.7.

55. Correct Answer: A
B is located at $-1\frac{2}{5}$ (-1.4).
Incorrect Answers:
B. *I* is located at 2.3.
C. *G* is located at $1\frac{1}{4}$ (1.25).
D. *A* is located at $-2\frac{1}{3}$ (-2.33...).

56. Correct Answer: B
J is located at $\frac{11}{4}$ (2.75 or $2\frac{3}{4}$).
Incorrect Answers:
A. *F* is located at $\frac{4}{5}$ (0.8).
C. *D* is located at $-\frac{4}{5}$ (-0.8).
D. 2.5 is not labeled on this number line.

Ordering Rational Numbers *(page 49)*

57. Correct Answer: A
-0.8, $-\frac{7}{8}$ (-0.875), $-\frac{10}{7}$ (-1.43), $-1\frac{5}{6}$ (-1.83) is in order from greatest to least.
Incorrect Answers:
B. $-\frac{7}{8}$ and -0.8 were reversed.
C. $-1\frac{5}{6}$ and $-\frac{10}{7}$ were reversed.
D. $-1\frac{5}{6}$, $-\frac{10}{7}$, $-\frac{7}{8}$, -0.8 is in order from least to greatest.

58. Correct Answer: C
2.35, $\frac{3}{5}$ (0.6), $-\frac{11}{6}$ (-1.83), -2.35 is in order from greatest to least.
Incorrect Answers:
A. 2.35, -2.35, $-\frac{11}{6}$, $\frac{3}{5}$ is in order according to the value of the numbers without considering the negative signs (according to the absolute values of the numbers).
B. -2.35, $-\frac{11}{6}$, $\frac{3}{5}$, 2.35 is in order from least to greatest.
D. -2.35 and 2.35 were reversed.

59. Correct Answer: D
-5.1, 0.13, $\frac{9}{10}$ (0.9), $2\frac{2}{3}$ (2.67) is in order from least to greatest.
Incorrect Answers:
A. $2\frac{2}{3}$, $\frac{9}{10}$, 0.13, -5.1 is in order from greatest to least.
B. $\frac{9}{10}$ and 0.13 were reversed.
C. -5.1 and $2\frac{2}{3}$ were reversed.

60. Correct Answer: B
$-3\frac{7}{9}$ (-3.78), $-\frac{15}{4}$ (-3.75), -3.4, 1.25 is in order from least to greatest.
Incorrect Answers:
A. 1.25, -3.4, $-\frac{15}{4}$, $-3\frac{7}{9}$ is in order from greatest to least.
C. $-3\frac{7}{9}$ and $-\frac{15}{4}$ were reversed.
D. 1.25 and -3.4 were reversed.

Absolute Value of Rational Numbers *(page 50)*

61. Correct Answer: D
H is eleven tic marks to the right of zero on the number line, so the integer naming *H* is 11. The absolute value (distance from zero) of 11 is 11.
Incorrect Answers:
A. *11* and *-11* represent the integer 11 and its opposite.
B. *-11* and *-11* represent the integer eleven tic marks to the *left* of zero.
C. *-11* and *11* represent the integer eleven tic marks to the *left* of zero and its absolute value.

Explanations for Test B Answers *(cont.)*

62. Correct Answer: C
C is nine tic marks to the left of zero on the number line, so the integer naming *C* is -9. The absolute value (distance from zero) of -9 is 9.
Incorrect Answers:
A. *9* and *9* represent the integer nine tic marks to the *right* of zero.
B. *-9* and *-9* both represent the integer naming *C*.
D. *9* and *-9* represent the integer nine tic marks to the *right* of zero and its opposite.

63. Correct Answer: A
20,320 feet above sea level is a positive integer: 20,320. The absolute value (distance from zero) of the integer is 20,320.
Incorrect Answers:
B. *-20,320* and *20,320* represent an elevation *below* sea level and that integer's absolute value.
C. *20,320* and *-20,320* represent the elevation of Mount McKinley and its opposite.
D. *-20,320* and *-20,320* both represent an elevation *below* sea level.

64. Correct Answer: C
8 feet *below* sea level is a negative integer: -8. The absolute value (distance from zero) of the integer is 8.
Incorrect Answers:
A. *-8* and *-8* both represent the elevation of New Orleans.
B. *8* and *-8* represent an elevation *above* sea level and that integer's opposite.
D. *8* and *8* both represent the absolute value of the elevation of New Orleans.

Expressions with Whole-number Exponents (page 51)

65. Correct Answer: C
The base (7) tells which number to use as a factor, and the exponent (3) tells how many times the base is used as a factor.
Incorrect Answers:
A. The base (7) was multiplied by the exponent (3).
B. The exponent (3) was incorrectly used as the base, and the base (7) was incorrectly used as the exponent.
D. *C* is correct, so *none of the above* is incorrect.

66. Correct Answer: D
$7^3 = 7 \times 7 \times 7 = 343$
Incorrect Answers:
A. The base (7) and the exponent (3) were added.
B. The base (7) was multiplied by the exponent (3).
C. The exponent (3) was incorrectly used as the base, and the base (7) was incorrectly used as the exponent.

67. Correct Answer: A
The base (5) tells which number to use as a factor, and the exponent (4) tells how many times the base is used as a factor.
Incorrect Answers:
B. The base (5) was multiplied by the exponent (4).
C. The exponent (4) was incorrectly used as the base, and the base (5) was incorrectly used as the exponent.
D. *A* is correct, so *none of the above* is incorrect.

68. Correct Answer: B
$5^4 = 5 \times 5 \times 5 \times 5 = 625$
Incorrect Answers:
A. The base (5) was multiplied by the exponent (4).
C. The exponent (4) was incorrectly used as the base, and the base (5) was incorrectly used as the exponent.
D. The base (5) and the exponent (4) were added.

Variable Expressions (page 52)

69. Correct Answer: B
Decreased by indicates subtraction (find the difference).
Incorrect Answers:
A. $x - 16$ represents *a number x decreased by 16.*
C. $16 + x$ represents *16 increased by a number x.*
D. $16 \div x$ represents *16 divided by a number x.*

70. Correct Answer: D
Quotient indicates division.
Incorrect Answers:
A. $2 \div c$ represents *the quotient of 2 divided by a number c.*
B. $c - 2$ is a *difference.*
C. $c + 2$ is a *sum.*

71. Correct Answer: A
Product indicates multiplication.
Incorrect Answers:
B. $9 + h$ is a *sum.*
C. $9 - h$ is a *difference.*
D. $9 \div h$ is a *quotient.*

72. Correct Answer: C
More than indicates addition (find the sum).
Incorrect Answers:
A. $12b$ represents *12 times a number b.*
B. $12 \div b$ represents *12 divided by a number b.*
D. $12 - b$ represents *a number b that is less than 12.*

Evaluating Expressions (page 53)

73. Correct Answer: B
Replace the variable *n* with 2: $2^4 + 3(3) + 3(2)$. Follow order of operations. *EXPONENTS:* $16 + 3(3) + 3(2)$.
MULTIPLY/DIVIDE: $16 + 9 + 6$.
ADD/SUBTRACT: $25 + 6 = 31$.
Incorrect Answers:
A. 2^4 was calculated as $2 \times 4 = 8$ instead of $2 \times 2 \times 2 \times 2 = 16$.
C. The order of operations was not followed; the expression was simplified from left to right.
D. *B* is correct, so *none of the above* is incorrect.

74. Correct Answer: C
Replace the variable *x* with 4: $4^3 - 3(5) + 4 \div 4$. Follow order of operations. *EXPONENTS:* $64 - 3(5) + 4 \div 4$.
MULTIPLY/DIVIDE: $64 - 15 + 1$.
ADD/SUBTRACT: $64 - 15 + 1 = 49 + 1 = 50$.
Incorrect Answers:
A. 4^3 was calculated as $4 \times 3 = 12$ instead of $4 \times 4 \times 4 = 64$. Then, 12 and 15 were subtracted in the wrong order.
B. The order of operations was not followed; the expression was simplified from left to right, except that $4 \div 4 = 1$ was calculated correctly.
D. *C* is correct, so *none of the above* is incorrect.

Explanations for Test B Answers *(cont.)*

75. Correct Answer: A
Replace the variable p with 3 since Seeta earned 3 points for each race: $2(3) + 4(3) + 2$. Multiply then add to find how many points she earned for the races: 6 points for the relay races + 12 points for the 50-metre dashes = 18 points. Add the 2 points for being voted outstanding new athlete: $18 + 2 = 20$.
Incorrect Answers:
- **B.** p was not replaced with 3; the existing numbers in the expression were added together.
- **C.** The term $+2$ was omitted when evaluating the expression.
- **D.** *A* is correct, so *none of the above* is incorrect.

76. Correct Answer: D
Replace the variable m with 30 since Satish drove 30 miles to work and 30 miles home from work: $2(30) + 10$. Multiply to find how many miles Satish drove to and from work, then add the 10 miles that he drove during lunch time:
$2(30) + 10 = 60 + 10 = 70$.
Incorrect Answers:
- **A.** The 10 miles that Satish drove during lunch time were not included.
- **B.** The given expression was not used to solve; all of the numbers given in the problem (30, 10, and 8) were added together.
- **C.** 78 miles includes the 8 miles that Satish *rode* with his friend.

Equivalent Expressions (page 54)

77. Correct Answer: C
Apply the distributive property by multiplying the term outside the parentheses by the terms inside the parentheses:
8 times $9x$ and 8 times $+ 9 = 72x + 72$.
Incorrect Answers:
- **A.** 8 and 9 were added instead of multiplied.
- **B.** 9 was not multiplied by 8.
- **D.** x was omitted from the answer.

78. Correct Answer: B
Apply the distributive property by multiplying the term outside the parentheses by the terms inside the parentheses:
6 times 7 and 6 times $+ 5y = 42 + 30y$.
Incorrect Answers:
- **A.** y was omitted from the answer.
- **C.** $5y$ was not multiplied by 6.
- **D.** 7 was not multiplied by 6.

79. Correct Answer: D
Use the distributive property in reverse to factor the expression. The greatest common factor of $49j$ and 42 is 7, so divide both terms by 7 to get $7(7j + 6)$.
Incorrect Answers:
- **A.** The second term inside parentheses should not have j: $7 \times 6j \neq 42$.
- **B.** The terms were incorrectly added together (unlike terms cannot be added).
- **C.** The variable j was omitted from the expression.

80. Correct Answer: C
Use the distributive property in reverse to factor the expression. The greatest common factor of $12g$ and 36 is 12, so divide both terms by 12 to get $12(g + 3)$.
Incorrect Answers:
- **A.** The terms were incorrectly added together (unlike terms cannot be added).
- **B.** The variable g was omitted from the expression.
- **D.** The second term inside parentheses should not have g; $12 \times 3g \neq 36$.

One-variable Equations and Inequalities (page 55)

81. Correct Answer: C
$(2 + 6) \times 4 = 8 \times 4 = 32$: $32 < 40$
Incorrect Answers:
- **A.** $(5 + 6) \times 4 = 11 \times 4 = 44$: $44 > 40$
- **B.** $(4 + 6) \times 4 = 10 \times 4 = 40$: $40 = 40$
- **D.** $(7 + 6) \times 4 = 13 \times 4 = 52$: $52 > 40$

82. Correct Answer: A
$46 - (3 \times 3) = 46 - 9 = 37$
Incorrect Answers:
- **B.** $31 - (3 \times 3) = 31 - 9 = 22$; $22 \neq 37$
- **C.** $28 - (3 \times 3) = 28 - 9 = 19$; $19 \neq 37$
- **D.** $40 - (3 \times 3) = 40 - 9 = 31$; $31 \neq 37$

83. Correct Answer: D
$(72 \div 8) - 7 = 9 - 7 = 2$
Incorrect Answers:
- **A.** $7 + (4 \times 5) = 7 + 20 = 27$; $27 < 29$
- **B.** $41 - 3(7) = 41 - 21 = 20$; $20 \neq 17$
- **C.** $6(7) + (3 \times 2) = 42 + 6 = 48$; $48 \neq 72$

84. Correct Answer: B
$4(9) - 8 = 36 - 8 = 28$
Incorrect Answers:
- **A.** $(45 \div 9) + 6 = 5 + 6 = 11$ and $3 \times 5 = 15$; $11 \neq 15$
- **C.** $2 + 7(9) = 2 + 63 = 65$; $65 \neq 58$
- **D.** $9 + 82 - 3 = 91 - 3 = 88$; $88 > 79$

Area (page 56)

85. Correct Answer: B
The area of the parallelogram is the area of the rectangle:
$A = bh = 6(3) = 18 \text{ ft.}^2$
Incorrect Answers:
- **A.** Only half of the length of the base of the parallelogram was used to solve.
- **C.** The area of the triangle was calculated.
- **D.** The label is incorrect; area is labeled in square units.

86. Correct Answer: D
$A = \frac{1}{2}h(b_1 + b_2) = \frac{1}{2}(12)(5 + 7) = 6(12) = 72 \text{ cm}^2$
Incorrect Answers:
- **A.** The label is incorrect.
- **B.** The height was not multiplied by $\frac{1}{2}$.
- **C.** The lengths of base_1 and base_2 were subtracted instead of added.

Explanations for Test B Answers *(cont.)*

87. Correct Answer: C
$A = \frac{1}{2}bh = \frac{1}{2}(16)(14) = 8(14) = 112 \text{ in.}^2$
Incorrect Answers:
- **A.** The label is incorrect; area is labeled in square units.
- **B.** The base was not multiplied by $\frac{1}{2}$.
- **D.** The base and the height were added together and then multiplied by $\frac{1}{2}$.

88. Correct Answer: C
$A = \frac{1}{2}bh = \frac{1}{2}(24)(8) = 12 \times 8 = 96 \text{ cm}^2$
Incorrect Answers:
- **A.** The base was not multiplied by $\frac{1}{2}$.
- **B.** The base and the height were added together and then multiplied by $\frac{1}{2}$.
- **D.** The label is incorrect; area is labeled in square units.

Volume of Rectangular Prisms with Fractional Sides (page 57)

89. Correct Answer: D
$V = l \times w \times h = 3\frac{1}{2} \times 2 \times 3 = \frac{7}{2} \times 2 \times 3 = 21 \text{ in.}^3$
Incorrect Answers:
- **A.** The wrong operation (addition) was used.
- **B.** The label is incorrect; volume is labeled in cubic units.
- **C.** An error occurred when simplifying after multiplying: $\frac{7}{2} \times 2$: $\frac{14}{2} \neq 8$.

90. Correct Answer: C
$V = l \times w \times h = 2\frac{1}{2} \times 2 \times 4 = \frac{5}{2} \times 2 \times 4 = 5 \times 4 = 20 \text{ cm}^3$
Incorrect Answers:
- **A.** The label is incorrect; volume is labeled in cubic units.
- **B.** An error occurred when simplifying after multiplying $\frac{5}{2} \times 2$: $\frac{10}{2} \neq 4$.
- **D.** The wrong operation (addition) was used.

91. Correct Answer: B
$V = l \times w \times h = 5\frac{1}{4} \times 3 \times 4 = \frac{21}{4} \times 4 \times 3 = 21 \times 3 = 63 \text{ ft.}^3$
Incorrect Answers:
- **A.** The wrong operation (addition) was used.
- **C.** An error occurred when simplifying after multiplying $\frac{21}{4} \times 4$: $\frac{84}{4} \neq 20$.
- **D.** The label is incorrect; volume is labeled in cubic units.

92. Correct Answer: D
$V = l \times w \times h = 3\frac{1}{3} \times 3 \times 3 = \frac{10}{3} \times 3 \times 3 = 10 \times 3 = 30 \text{ m}^3$
Incorrect Answers:
- **A.** The label is incorrect; volume is labeled in cubic units.
- **B.** An error occurred when simplifying after multiplying: $\frac{10}{3} \times 3$: $\frac{30}{3} \neq 3$.
- **C.** The wrong opperation (addition) was used.

Dot Plots (page 58)

93. Correct Answer: C
15 + 7 + 4 + 8 + 5 + 4 + 5 + 6 + 5 + 14 + 15 = 88 hours
Incorrect Answers:
- **A.** 80 hours does not include 8 hours for Betsy.
- **B.** 84 hours does not include 4 hours each for Devin and Mia.
- **D.** 11 is the number of students surveyed.

94. Correct Answer: D
mean = (15 + 7 + 4 + 8 + 5 + 4 + 5 + 6 + 5 + 14 + 15) ÷ 11 = 88 ÷ 11 = 8
Incorrect Answers:
- **A.** The label is incorrect.
- **B.** 88 is the total number of hours; it needs to be divided by 11 to find the mean.
- **C.** 6 is the median number of hours spent studying.

95. Correct Answer: B
Order the values from least to greatest:
4, 4, 5, 5, 5, ***6***, 7, 8, 14, 15, 15. 6 is the median.
Incorrect Answers:
- **A.** 5 is the number that occurs most often (mode).
- **C.** 4 is the least value.
- **D.** 8 is the mean.

96. Correct Answer: C
There is no noticeable shape. The height of the dots varies.
Incorrect Answers:
- **A.** The data on the right is not the highest amounts of dots, so it is not spread out to the right.
- **B.** The data on the left is not the highest amounts of dots, so it is not spread out to the left.
- **D.** The data's shape is not symmetric.

Histograms and Box Plots (page 59)

97. Correct Answer: D
41–45 minutes is an outlier because it is separated from the rest of the data by a gap from 26 to 40.
Incorrect Answers:
- **A.** 1–5 minutes is not an outlier; it is in a grouping with the rest of the data.
- **B.** 26–30 minutes is not an outlier; it falls in a gap of data.
- **C.** 36–40 minutes is not an outlier; it falls in a gap of data.

98. Correct Answer: C
The median is the point marked in the middle of the box of the box plot. To calculate median from the given values, order the values from least to greatest: 1, 2, 3, 3, 5, 6, 7, 7, 8, 8. Since there is an even number of data values, the median is the mean of the middle two numbers:
median = (5 + 6) ÷ 2 = 11 ÷ 2 = 5.5.
Incorrect Answers:
- **A.** 5 is one of the numbers in the middle of the data, but it is not *the* middle value.
- **B.** 6 is one of the numbers in the middle of the data, but it is not *the* middle value.
- **D.** 5 and 6 are the numbers in the middle of the list, and their mean is the median.

99. Correct Answer: A
Calculate the mean: mean =
(1 + 2 + 3 + 3 + 5 + 6 + 7 + 7 + 8 + 8) ÷ 10 = 50 ÷ 10 = 5.
Then calculate the difference between the mean and each data value: 5 – 1 = *4*; 5 – 2 = *3*; 5 – 3 = *2*; 5 – 3 = *2*; 5 – 5 = *0*; 6 – 5 = *1*; 7 – 5 = *2*; 7 – 5 = *2*; 8 – 5 = *3*; 8 – 5 = *3*.
Finally, calculate the mean of the differences:
mean absolute deviation =
(4 + 3 + 2 + 2 + 0 + 1 + 2 + 2 + 3 + 3) ÷ 10 = 22 ÷ 10 = 2.2.
Incorrect Answers:
- **B.** 22 is the total of the differences.
- **C.** 5 is the mean.
- **D.** 5.5 is the median.

100. Correct Answer: B
7 (3rd quartile) – 3 (1st quartile) = 4
Incorrect Answers:
- **A.** 7 is the 3rd quartile.
- **C.** 6 was calculated by subtracting the least value (1) from the 3rd quartile (7).
- **D.** 1 was calculated by subtracting the 3rd quartile (7) from the greatest value (8).

Explanations for Test C Answers

Ratios (page 60)

1. Correct Answer: C
There are 2 squares and 4 triangles; the ratio of squares to triangles can be written 2:4, $\frac{2}{4}$, or 2 to 4.
Incorrect Answers:
A. 4:2, $\frac{4}{2}$, and 4 to 2 represent the ratio of triangles to squares.
B. 2:6, $\frac{2}{6}$, and 2 to 6 represent the ratio of squares to circles.
D. 2:12, $\frac{2}{12}$, and 2 to 12 represent the ratio of squares to the total number of shapes.

2. Correct Answer: D
There are 12 shapes in all and 6 circles; the ratio of shapes to circles can be written 12:6, $\frac{12}{6}$, or 12 to 6.
Incorrect Answers:
A. 12:2, $\frac{12}{2}$, and 12 to 2 represent the ratio of total number of shapes to the number of squares.
B. 6:12, $\frac{6}{12}$, and 6 to 12 represent the ratio of circles to the total number of shapes.
C. 12:4, $\frac{12}{4}$, and 12 to 4 represent the ratio of total number of shapes to triangles.

3. Correct Answer: B
Compare the number of meat lover's pizzas (3) to the total number of pizzas (10) to find the ratio of meat lover's pizzas to the total number of pizzas (3:10).
Incorrect Answers:
A. 3:1 represents the ratio of meat lover's pizzas to vegetarian pizzas.
C. 3:2 represents the ratio of meat lover's pizzas to cheese pizzas.
D. 10:3 represents the ratio of of total number of pizzas to meat lover's pizzas.

4. Correct Answer: A
Compare the number of red beads (16) to the number of blue beads (14) to find the ratio of red beads to blue beads.
Incorrect Answers:
B. 14:16 represents the ratio of blue beads to red beads.
C. 16:15 represents the ratio of red beads to white beads.
D. 16:45 represents the ratio of red beads to total number of beads.

Ratio Relationships (page 61)

5. Correct Answer: D
Start with the ratio 8:6. Rewrite the ratio as a fraction: $\frac{8}{6}$. Since $6 \times 4 = 24$, multiply the numerator and denominator of the fraction by 4 to complete the ratio table: $\frac{8}{6} = \frac{32}{24}$.
Incorrect Answers:
A. The numbers were transposed when recording the answer.
B. 4 was added to the previous number in the column (24).
C. 4 was subtracted from the next number in the column (40).

6. Correct Answer: C
Start with the ratio 6:4. Rewrite the ratio as a fraction: $\frac{6}{4}$. Since $6 \times 3 = 18$, multiply the numerator and denominator of the fraction by 3 to complete the ratio table: $\frac{6}{4} = \frac{18}{12}$.
Incorrect Answers:
A. 3 was added to the previous number in the column (8).
B. 3 was subtracted from the next number in the column (16).
D. Since $18 + 6 = 24$ (in the first column), 6 was added to the previous number in the second column (8).

7. Correct Answer: D
The ratio of kilometres to gallons is $\frac{120}{8}$. To find an equivalent fraction with a numerator of 600 (600 kilometres), multiply the numerator and denominator by 5: $\frac{120}{8} = \frac{600}{40}$.
Incorrect Answers:
A. 120 was divided by 8; the fraction was simplified instead of finding an equivalent fraction.
B. The values in the ratio were reversed; the first term for kilometres was listed as 8 and the first term for gallons was listed as 120.
C. The right column was increased by 1 gallon of petrol in each row of the table until 600 kilometres was reached in the left column of the table.

8. Correct Answer: B
The ratio of white cars to minutes is $\frac{8}{6}$. To find an equivalent fraction with a denominator of 30 (30 minutes), multiply the numerator and denominator by 5: $\frac{8}{6} = \frac{40}{30}$.
Incorrect Answers:
A. The values in the ratio were reversed; the first term for white cars was listed as 6 and the first term for minutes was listed as 8.
C. The first value in the left column (white cars) was incorrectly written as 16 instead of 8, and the values in the left column increased by 16 instead of 8.
D. The values in the left column (white cars) were increased by 1 until the right column reached 30 minutes.

Unit Rate Ratios (page 62)

9. Correct Answer: C
Write the amount of money over the number of pieces to find the rate: $\frac{₹7.92}{6\text{ pieces}}$. The fraction bar indicates division, so divide the amount (₹7.92) by the number of pieces (6) to find the unit rate: $\frac{₹1.32}{1\text{piece}}$. The second number of a unit rate is always 1.
Incorrect Answers:
A. A division error occurred when finding the unit rate, and the denominator was not changed to 1 after dividing.
B. The denominator was not changed to 1 after dividing.
D. *C* is correct, so *none of the above* is incorrect.

10. Correct Answer: D
Write the number of roses over the number of vases to find the rate: $\frac{48\text{ roses}}{6\text{ vases}}$. The fraction bar indicates division, so divide the number of roses (48) by the number of vases (6) to find the unit rate: $\frac{8\text{ roses}}{1\text{ vase}}$.
Incorrect Answers:
A. The values were reversed when writing the rate, so the unit rate is also incorrect.
B. The denominator was not changed to 1 after dividing.
C. A division error occurred when finding the unit rate.

11. Correct Answer: B
Write the number of races over the number of weeks to find the rate: $\frac{28\text{ races}}{7\text{ weeks}}$. The fraction bar indicates division, so divide the number of races (28) by the number of weeks (7) to find the unit rate: $\frac{4\text{ races}}{1\text{ week}}$ or 4 races per week.
Incorrect Answers:
A. The denominator was not changed to 1 after dividing.
C. A division error occurred when finding the unit rate.
D. The values were reversed when writing the rate, so the unit rate is also incorrect.

Explanations for Test C Answers *(cont.)*

12. Correct Answer: C

Write the number of words Kala can type over the number of minutes to find the rate: $\frac{1{,}200 \text{ words}}{20 \text{ minutes}}$. The fraction bar indicates division, so divide the number of words (1,200) by the number of minutes (20) to find the unit rate: $\frac{60 \text{ words}}{1 \text{ minute}}$ or 60 words per minute.

Incorrect Answers:

A. A division error occurred when finding the unit rate.

B. The rate was written correctly ($\frac{1{,}200 \text{ words}}{20 \text{ minutes}}$), but the wrong operation (multiplication) was used to find the unit rate.

D. The question was not interpreted correctly. The answer, 20, represents the amount of time only.

Percent (page 63)

13. Correct Answer: C

$30\% = \frac{30}{100}$. *Of* means *multiply:* $\frac{30}{100} \times \frac{200}{1}$. Cross-cancel 100 and 200 to get $\frac{30}{1} \times \frac{2}{1} = \frac{60}{1} = 60$.

Incorrect Answers:

A. 30% was incorrectly written as $\frac{30}{10}$.

B. 30% was incorrectly written as $\frac{30}{1{,}000}$.

D. An error occurred when multiplying the fractions: ($\frac{30}{100} \times \frac{200}{1} \neq \frac{30}{1}$).

14. Correct Answer: B

$55\% = \frac{55}{100}$. *Of* means *multiply:* $\frac{55}{100} \times \frac{500}{1}$.
Cross-cancel to get $\frac{55}{1} \times \frac{5}{1} = \frac{275}{1} = 275$.

Incorrect Answers:

A. 55% was incorrectly written as $\frac{55}{1{,}000}$.

C. 55% was incorrectly written as $\frac{50}{100}$.

D. 55% was incorrectly written as $\frac{55}{10}$.

15. Correct Answer: D

$20\% = \frac{20}{100} = 0.2$. Multiply to find 20% of the cost of the rose bush: $0.2 \times 36.50 =$ ₹7.30.

Incorrect Answers:

A. 20% was incorrectly written as $\frac{20}{10}$.

B. ₹29.20 is the final price for the bush after the discount.

C. 20% was incorrectly written as $\frac{20}{1{,}000}$.

16. Correct Answer: A

$25\% = \frac{25}{100}$. Multiply to find 25% *of* Nitin's workday:
$\frac{25}{100} \times \frac{8}{1} = \frac{200}{100} = 2$ hours.

Incorrect Answers:

B. 10 is the number of hours Nitin works plus the number of hours he rides on the train.

C. 25% was incorrectly written as $\frac{100}{25}$.

D. 25% was incorrectly written as $\frac{25}{1{,}000}$.

Dividing Fractions (page 64)

17. Correct Answer: D

Change division to multiplication, and change the divisor to its reciprocal: $\frac{1}{3} \times \frac{9}{5} = \frac{9}{15} = \frac{3}{5}$.

Incorrect Answers:

A. The answer was not simplified.

B. Division was changed to multiplication, but the divisor was not changed to its reciprocal.

C. The dividend was changed to its reciprocal instead of the divisor.

18. Correct Answer: B

Change division to multiplication, and change the divisor to its reciprocal: $\frac{2}{5} \times \frac{3}{2} = \frac{6}{10} = \frac{3}{5}$.

Incorrect Answers:

A. The dividend was changed to its reciprocal instead of the divisor.

C. Division was changed to multiplication, but the divisor was not changed to its reciprocal.

D. The answer was not simplified.

19. Correct Answer: C

Divide the total amount of land by $\frac{1}{8}$-acre per parcel to find how many parcels of land Raju will have: $\frac{3}{4} \div \frac{1}{8} = \frac{3}{4} \times \frac{8}{1} = \frac{24}{4} = 6$.

Incorrect Answers:

A. The answer was not simplified.

B. Division was changed to multiplication, but the divisor was not changed to its reciprocal.

D. The dividend was changed to its reciprocal instead of the divisor.

20. Correct Answer: A

Divide the total amount of sauce Raj made by $\frac{1}{3}$-litre servings to find how many servings of sauce he made:
$\frac{3}{4} \div \frac{1}{3} = \frac{3}{4} \times \frac{3}{1} = \frac{9}{4} = 2\frac{1}{4}$.

Incorrect Answers:

B. Division was changed to multiplication, but the divisor was not changed to its reciprocal.

C. The dividend was changed to its reciprocal instead of the divisor.

D. Both the dividend and the divisor were changed to their reciprocals.

Dividing Multi-digit Numbers (page 65)

21. Correct Answer: B

6,885 ÷ 367 = 18 R279
Check: 18 × 367 = 6,606; 6,606 + 279 = 6,885

Incorrect Answers:

A. The quotient and the remainder were reversed.

C. The remainder was not included in the answer.

D. In the second division step, 367 divides into 3,215 eight times, not seven.

22. Correct Answer: C

7,346 ÷ 15 = 489 R11
Check: 489 × 15 = 7,335; 7,335 + 11 = 7,346

Incorrect Answers:

A. The remainder was not included in the answer.

B. In the third division step, the 9 was not written in the quotient.

D. In the third division step, 15 divides into 146 nine times, not eight.

23. Correct Answer: D

3,064 ÷ 48 = 63 R40
Check: 63 × 48 = 3,024; 3,024 + 40 = 3,064

Incorrect Answers:

A. In the second division step, 48 divides into 184 three times, not two.

B. In the second subtraction step, the numbers in the ones column were not subtracted.

C. The remainder was not included in the answer.

Explanations for Test C Answers *(cont.)*

24. Correct Answer: A
9,450 birds ÷ 175 areas = 54 birds per area
Incorrect Answers:
B. 4 should be in the ones place in the quotient, not written as the remainder.
C. In the second division step, 175 divides into 700 four times not three.
D. *Areas* is the wrong label.

Adding, Subtracting, Multiplying, and Dividing Decimals (page 66)

25. Correct Answer: C
Move the decimal point in the divisor until it becomes a whole number; move the decimal point in the dividend the same number of places, and divide: 66.15 ÷ 0.63 = 105.0.
Incorrect Answers:
A. A zero should have been written in the tens place of the quotient.
B. The decimal point is in the wrong place.
D. The decimal point is in the wrong place.

26. Correct Answer: D
Align the decimal points before subtracting:
6.269 – 0.8 = 5.469.
Incorrect Answers:
A. A comma was used instead of a decimal point.
B. The decimal points were not aligned before subtracting; the numbers were aligned flush right.
C. The decimal point is in the wrong place.

27. Correct Answer: A
Align the decimal points before adding: 56.1 + 24.742 = 80.842.
Incorrect Answers:
B. The decimal point is in the wrong place.
C. The decimal point is in the wrong place.
D. The decimal points were not aligned before adding; the numbers were aligned flush right.

28. Correct Answer: C
Align the factors on the right; place the decimal point in the product after multiplying: 9.17 × 4.33 = 39.7061.
Incorrect Answers:
A. The decimal point is in the wrong place.
B. The decimal point is in the wrong place.
D. The decimal point is in the wrong place.

Greatest Common Factor of Two Whole Numbers (page 67)

29. Correct Answer: B
Factors of 21: 1, 3, <u>*7*</u>, 21
Factors of 49: 1, <u>*7*</u>, 49
GCF = 7
Incorrect Answers:
A. 2 is not a factor of 21 or 49.
C. 21 is a factor of 21 but is not a factor of 49.
D. 3 is a factor of 21 but is not a factor of 49.

30. Correct Answer: D
Factors of 12: 1, 2, 3, 4, 6, <u>*12*</u>
Factors of 36: 1, 2, 3, 4, 6, 9, <u>*12*</u>, 18, 36
GCF = 12
Incorrect Answers:
A. 4 is not the *greatest* common factor.
B. 3 is not the *greatest* common factor.
C. 6 is not the *greatest* common factor.

31. Correct Answer: C
Factors of 18: 1, 2, 3, <u>*6*</u>, 9, 18
Factors of 42: 1, 2, 3, <u>*6*</u>, 7, 14, 21, 42
GCF = 6, not 3
Incorrect Answers:
A. Factors of 6: 1, 2, <u>*3*</u>, 6
Factors of 21: 1, <u>*3*</u>, 7, 21
GCF = 3
B. Factors of 12: 1, 2, <u>*3*</u>, 4, 6, 12
Factors of 63: 1, <u>*3*</u>, 7, 9, 21, 63
GCF = 3
D. Factors of 15: 1, <u>*3*</u>, 5, 15
Factors of 24: 1, 2, <u>*3*</u>, 4, 6, 8, 12, 24
GCF = 3

32. Correct Answer: A
Factors of 36: 1, 2, 3, 4, 6, 9, <u>*12*</u>, 18, 36
Factors of 48: 1, 2, 3, 4, 6, 8, <u>*12*</u>, 16, 24, 48
GCF = 12
Incorrect Answers:
B. Factors of 8: 1, 2, 4, <u>*8*</u>
Factors of 16: 1, 2, 4, <u>*8*</u>, 16
GCF = 8, not 4
C. Factors of 14: 1, 2, <u>*7*</u>, 14
Factors of 35: 1, 5, <u>*7*</u>, 35
GCF = 7, not 5
D. Factors of 56: 1, 2, 4, 7, <u>*8*</u>, 14, 28, 56
Factors of 64: 1, 2, 4, <u>*8*</u>, 16, 32, 64
GCF = 8, not 4

Least Common Multiple of Two Whole Numbers (page 68)

33. Correct Answer: C
Multiples of 3: 3, 6, 9, <u>*12*</u>, 15, 18, 21, 24, 27, 30, 33, 36, 39, 42, 45, 48, …
Multiples of 12: <u>*12*</u>, 24, 36, 48, 60, …
LCM = 12
Incorrect Answers:
A. 36 is not the *least* common multiple.
B. 24 is not the *least* common multiple.
D. 48 is not the *least* common multiple.

34. Correct Answer: A
Multiples of 5: 5, <u>*10*</u>, 15, 20, 25, 30, 35, …
Multiples of 10: <u>*10*</u>, 20, 30, 40, 50, 60, 70, …
LCM = 10
Incorrect Answers:
B. 35 is a multiple of 5 but is not a multiple of 10.
C. 20 is not the *least* common multiple.
D. 30 is not the *least* common multiple.

Explanations for Test C Answers *(cont.)*

35. Correct Answer: D
Multiples of 8: 8, 16, 24, 32, 40, 48, 56, 64, *72*, ...
Multiples of 9: 9, 18, 27, 36, 45, 54, 63, *72*, ...
LCM = 72
Incorrect Answers:
A. Multiples of 3: 3, 6, *9*, 12, 15, 18, ...
Multiples of 9: *9*, 18, 27, 36, 45, 54, ...
LCM = 9, not 18
B. Multiples of 6: 6, 12, 18, 24, 30, 36, *42*, 48, 54, 60, 66, 72, 78, 84, ...
Multiples of 7: 7, 14, 21, 28, 35, *42*, 49, 56, 63, 70, 77, 84, ...; LCM = 42, not 84
C. Multiples of 2: 2, 4, 6, *8*, 10, 12, 14, 16, 18, 20, 22, 24, ...
Multiples of 8: *8*, 16, 24, ...
LCM = 8, not 24

36. Correct Answer: C
Multiples of 4: 4, 8, *12*, ...
Multiples of 6: 6, *12*, ...
LCM = 12
Incorrect Answers:
A. Multiples of 9: 9, 18, 27, *36*, ...
Multiples of 12: 12, 24, *36*, ...
LCM = 36, not 12
B. Multiples of 11: 11, 22, 33, 44, 55, 66, 77, 88, 99, 110, 121, *132*, ...
Multiples of 12: 12, 24, 36, 48, 60, 72, 84, 96, 108, 120, *132*, ...
LCM = 132, not 12
D. Multiples of 3: 3, 6, 9, 12, 15, 18, 21, *24*, ...
Multiples of 8: 8, 16, *24*, ...
LCM = *24*, not 12

Distributive Property (page 69)

37. Correct Answer: C
48 + 16 = *64* and (8 × 6) + (8 × 2) = 48 + 16 = *64*
Incorrect Answers:
A. 8(6 × 2) = 8(12) = 96; 96 ≠ 64
B. 6(8 × 3) = 6(24) = 144; 144 ≠ 64
D. (8 + 6) × (8 + 2) = 14 × 10 = 140; 140 ≠ 64

38. Correct Answer: B
32 + 8 = *40* and 4(8 + 2) = (4 × 8) + (4 × 2) = 32 + 8 = *40*
Incorrect Answers:
A. 4(8 × 2) = 4(16) = 64; 64 ≠ 40
C. (4 × 8) × (4 × 2) = 32 × 8 = 256; 256 ≠ 40
D. 8(4 + 2) = (8 × 4) + (8 × 2) = 32 + 16 = 48; 48 ≠ 40

39. Correct Answer: D
56 + 28 = *84* and 7(8 + 4) = (7 × 8) + (7 × 4) = 56 + 28 = *84*
Incorrect Answers:
A. *8*(8 + 4) = (8 × 8) + (8 × 4) = 64 + 32 = 96; 96 ≠ 84
B. *6*(8 + 4) = (6 × 8) + (6 × 4) = 48 + 24 = 72; 72 ≠ 84
C. *9*(8 + 4) = (9 × 8) + (9 × 4) = 72 + 36 = 108; 108 ≠ 84

40. Correct Answer: C
(3 × 7) + (3 × 6) = 21 + 18 = *39* and 3(7 + 6) = (3 × 7) + (3 × 6) = 21 + 18 = *39*
Incorrect Answers:
A. 3(7 × 6) = 3(42) = 126; 126 ≠ 39
B. 21 × 18 = 378; 378 ≠ 39; the original expression is equal to 21 + 18, not 21 × 18.
D. 7(3 + 6) = (7 × 3) + (7 × 6) = 21 + 42 = 63; 63 ≠ 39

Positive and Negative Numbers (page 70)

41. Correct Answer: D
highest = 26 feet above sea level = 26; lowest = 5 feet below sea level = -5
Incorrect Answers:
A. -26 represents 26 below sea level, not 26 above.
B. The highest and lowest values are reversed.
C. 5 represents 5 above sea level, not 5 below.

42. Correct Answer: A
(Atlantic City) 31 above = 31; 31 is the greatest integer.
Incorrect Answers:
B. Spray Beach's highest tide is 26: 26 < 31.
C. Point Pleasant's highest tide is 8: 8 < 31.
D. Seaside's highest tide is 15: 15 < 31.

43. Correct Answer: B
Brigantine's highest tide is 7 and its lowest tide is -7: 7 and -7 are opposite integers.
Incorrect Answers:
A. Seaside's highest tide is 15 and its lowest is -10: 15 and -10 are not opposite integers.
C. Point Pleasant's highest tide is 8 and its lowest is -12: 8 and -12 are not opposite integers.
D. Atlantic City's highest tide is 31 and its lowest is -1: 31 and -1 are not opposite integers.

44. Correct Answer: C
highest = 8 above sea level = 8; lowest = 12 below sea level = -12
Incorrect Answers:
A. The highest and lowest values are reversed.
B. 12 represents 12 above sea level, not 12 below.
D. -8 represents 8 below sea level, not 8 above; 12 represents 12 above sea level, not 12 below.

Numbers and Their Opposites (page 71)

45. Correct Answer: D
The opposite of a positive integer is a negative integer, so the opposite of 4 is -4 (*C*).
Incorrect Answers:
A. *B* = -5
B. *D* = -1
C. *G* = 4

46. Correct Answer: B
The opposite of a negative integer is a positive integer, so the opposite of -1 is 1 (*E*).
Incorrect Answers:
A. *F* = 2
C. *A* = -9
D. *H* = 8

47. Correct Answer: C
The opposite of 12 is -12.
Incorrect Answers:
A. This would be 12.
B. This would be $\frac{1}{12}$.
D. This would be $-\frac{1}{12}$.

Explanations for Test C Answers *(cont.)*

48. Correct Answer: C
The opposite of the opposite is the number itself: -(-6) = 6.
Incorrect Answers:
A. (-6) = -6; it does not equal -(-6).
B. 12 = 12; it does not equal -(-6).
D. -6 = -6; it does not equal -(-6).

Ordered Pairs on a Coordinate Plane (page 72)

49. Correct Answer: C
F is located four spaces to the left of zero on the *x*-axis and eight spaces below zero on the *y*-axis: (-4,-8).
Incorrect Answers:
A. *B* = (-4,8)
B. *C* = (-5,-7)
D. *H* = (-1,6)

50. Correct Answer: A
D is located two spaces to the right of zero on the *x*-axis and six spaces below zero on the *y*-axis: (2,-6).
Incorrect Answers:
B. *H* = (-1,6)
C. *G* = (6,1)
D. *A* = (-3,1)

51. Correct Answer: B
E is located three spaces to the right of zero on the *x*-axis and two spaces below zero on the *y*-axis: (3,-2).
Incorrect Answers:
A. (6,1) is *G*.
C. (-4,8) is *B*.
D. (-3,1) is *A*.

52. Correct Answer: D
C is located five spaces to the left of zero on the *x*-axis and seven spaces below zero on the *y*-axis: (-5,-7).
Incorrect Answers:
A. (-1,6) is *H*.
B. (-3,1) is *A*.
C. (-4,-8) is *F*.

Identifying Rational Numbers on a Number Line (page 73)

53. Correct Answer: A
D is located at $-\frac{5}{10}$ (-0.5).
Incorrect Answers:
B. *F* is located at $\frac{1}{2}$ (0.5).
C. *E* is located at -0.125.
D. *B* is located at -1.9.

54. Correct Answer: B
I is located at 2.8.
Incorrect Answers:
A. *A* is located at -2.6.
C. *H* is located at 1.8.
D. *C* is located at -1.8.

55. Correct Answer: D
H is located at $1\frac{4}{5}$ (1.8).
Incorrect Answers:
A. *G* is located at 0.7.
B. *C* is located at $-\frac{9}{5}$ (-1.8).
C. *B* is located at -1.9.

56. Correct Answer: C
A is located at -2.6.
Incorrect Answers:
A. 2.6 is a positive number. *A* is located on the opposite side of the number line.
B. *B* is located at -1.9.
D. *D* is located at $-\frac{5}{10}$.

Ordering Rational Numbers (page 74)

57. Correct Answer: D
1.45, 1.4, $\frac{5}{6}$ (0.83), -1.45 is in order from greatest to least.
Incorrect Answers:
A. -1.45 and 1.45 are reversed.
B. -1.45, $\frac{5}{6}$, 1.4, 1.45 is in order from least to greatest.
C. $\frac{5}{6}$ and 1.4 are reversed.

58. Correct Answer: C
-0.33, $-\frac{5}{4}$ (-1.25), -1.6, $-1\frac{5}{8}$ (-1.625) is in order from greatest to least.
Incorrect Answers:
A. $-1\frac{5}{8}$, -1.6, $-\frac{5}{4}$, -0.33 is in order from least to greatest.
B. -1.6 and $-1\frac{5}{8}$ are reversed.
D. $-\frac{5}{4}$ and -0.33 are reversed.

59. Correct Answer: C
$-\frac{14}{3}$ (-4.67), -4.17, $1\frac{2}{5}$ (1.4), 2.7 is in order from least to greatest.
Incorrect Answers:
A. 2.7 and $-\frac{14}{3}$ are reversed.
B. 2.7 and $1\frac{2}{5}$ are reversed.
D. 2.7, $1\frac{2}{5}$, -4.17, $-\frac{14}{3}$ is in order from greatest to least.

60. Correct Answer: A
-2.3, $-2\frac{1}{9}$ (-2.11), $-\frac{2}{7}$ (-0.29), $\frac{2}{7}$ (0.29) is in order from least to greatest.
Incorrect Answers:
B. $\frac{2}{7}$, $-\frac{2}{7}$, $-2\frac{1}{9}$, -2.3 is in order from greatest to least.
C. $\frac{2}{7}$ and $-\frac{2}{7}$ are reversed.
D. $\frac{2}{7}$ is the greatest, not the least.

Absolute Value of Rational Numbers (page 75)

61. Correct Answer: C
G is eight tic marks to the right of zero on the number line, so the integer naming *G* is 8. The absolute value (distance from zero) of 8 is 8.
Incorrect Answers:
A. *-8* and *8* represent the integer eight tic marks to the *left* of zero and its opposite.
B. *7* is the wrong integer.
D. *8* and *-8* represent the integer 8 and its opposite.

62. Correct Answer: D
D is five tic marks to the left of zero on the number line, so the integer naming *D* is -5. The absolute value (distance from zero) of -5 is 5.
Incorrect Answers:
A. *-4* is the wrong integer.
B. *-5* and *-5* both represent the integer naming *D*.
C. *5* and *5* represent the integer five tic marks to the *right* of zero and its absolute value.

Explanations for Test C Answers (cont.)

63. **Correct Answer: A**
80° *below* zero is a negative integer: -80. The absolute value (distance from zero) of the integer is 80.
Incorrect Answers:
B. *80* and *-80* represent 80° *above* zero and its opposite.
C. *80* and *80* both represent 80° *above* zero.
D. *-80* and *-80* both represent 80° below zero.

64. **Correct Answer: D**
One hundred thirty-four degrees is a positive integer: 134. The absolute value (distance from zero) of the integer is 134.
Incorrect Answers:
A. *-134* and *134* represent 134° *below* zero and its absolute value.
B. *134* and *-134* represent 134° and its opposite.
C. *-134* and *-134* both represent 134° *below* zero.

Expressions with Whole-number Exponents (page 76)

65. **Correct Answer: C**
The base (3) tells which number to use as a factor, and the exponent (5) tells how many times the base is used as a factor.
Incorrect Answers:
A. The base (3) was multiplied by the exponent (5).
B. The exponent (5) was incorrectly used as the base, and the base (3) was incorrectly used as the exponent.
D. *C* is correct, so *none of the above* is incorrect.

66. **Correct Answer: D**
$3^5 = 3 \times 3 \times 3 \times 3 \times 3 = 243$
Incorrect Answers:
A. The exponent (5) was incorrectly used as the base, and the base (3) was incorrectly used as the exponent.
B. The base (3) was multiplied by the exponent (5).
C. The exponent was added to the base.

67. **Correct Answer: A**
The base (2) tells which number to use as a factor, and the exponent (6) tells how many times the base is used as a factor.
Incorrect Answers:
B. The base (2) was multiplied by the exponent (6).
C. The exponent (6) was incorrectly used as the base, and the base (2) was incorrectly used as the exponent.
D. *A* is correct, so *none of the above* is incorrect.

68. **Correct Answer: B**
$2^6 = 2 \times 2 \times 2 \times 2 \times 2 \times 2 = 64$
Incorrect Answers:
A. The base and the exponent were multiplied.
C. The exponent (6) was incorrectly used as the base, and the base (2) was incorrectly used as the exponent.
D. The base (2) and the exponent (6) were added.

Variable Expressions (page 77)

69. **Correct Answer: B**
Divided into indicates division. *Into* reverses the order of the terms when writing the expression.
Incorrect Answers:
A. *26n* is 26 *times* or *multiplied by a number n.*
C. $n \div 26$ represents *26 divided into a number n.*
D. $n + 26$ represents *a number n added to 26.*

70. **Correct Answer: A**
t tickets at ₹12 each means that ₹12 is being spent for each ticket that is purchased, or ₹12 is being paid *t* times (a *product*).
Incorrect Answers:
B. $t - 12$ is a *difference.*
C. $t + 12$ is a *sum.*
D. $t \div 12$ is a *quotient.*

71. **Correct Answer: D**
Fewer than indicates subtraction. *Than* indicates that the order of the terms in the algebraic expression must be reversed from the order in which the terms are written in the word expression.
Incorrect Answers:
A. $16r$ represents *16 times r.*
B. $r \div 16$ represents *r divided by 16.*
C. $r - 16$ represents *16 fewer than r.*

72. **Correct Answer: B**
Twice represents *two times* (multiply by two).
Incorrect Answers:
A. $2 + h$ represents *two plus a number h.*
C. $2 - h$ represents *two minus a number h.*
D. $2 \div h$ represents *two divided by a number h.*

Evaluating Expressions (page 78)

73. **Correct Answer: A**
Replace the variable *t* with 6: $6^2 - 2(2) + 6 \div 2$. Follow order of operations. *EXPONENTS:* $36 - 2(2) + 6 \div 2$.
MULTIPLY/DIVIDE: $36 - 4 + 3$.
ADD/SUBTRACT: $32 + 3 = 35$.
Incorrect Answers:
B. The last part of the expression, *+6÷2*, was omitted from the calculations.
C. 6^2 was calculated as $6 \times 2 = 12$ instead of $6 \times 6 = 36$.
D. *A* is correct, so *none of the above* is incorrect.

74. **Correct Answer: B**
Replace the variable *r* with 4: $4^3 + 52 \div 4$. Follow order of operations. *EXPONENTS:* $64 + 52 \div 4$.
MULTIPLY/DIVIDE: $64 + 13$.
ADD/SUBRTRACT: $64 + 13 = 77$.
Incorrect Answers:
A. 4^3 was incorrectly calculated as $4 \times 3 = 12$ instead of $4 \times 4 \times 4 = 64$.
C. The order of operations was not followed; the expression was simplified from left to right.
D. *B* is correct, so *none of the above* is incorrect.

75. **Correct Answer: C**
Replace *e* with 55 since Karan earns ₹55 for each day of babysitting (for 8 days): $8(55) + 2(25) \div 2$.
Multiply 8 × ₹55 to find how much she earned in regular pay (₹440).
Multiply 2 × ₹25 to find how much she earned in tips (₹50).
Divide the tips by 2 since she shares with her assistant: ₹50 ÷ 2 = ₹25 in tips.
Total earned = ₹440 + ₹25 = ₹465.
Incorrect Answers:
A. The ₹50 Karan earned in tips was not divided by two.
B. An error occurred when multiplying: $55 \times 8 \neq 400$.
D. The order of operations was not followed; the expression was simplified from left to right.

Explanations for Test C Answers *(cont.)*

76. Correct Answer: D
Replace *h* with 3 since it took the repairman 3 hours to repair the machine:
65 + 35(3) + 54. Multiply 35 × 3 to find how much Kala will pay for the hourly service (₹105). Add the inspection fee, the hourly cost, and the cost for the part to find the total:
65 + 105 + 54 = ₹224.
Incorrect Answers:
A. The order of operations was not followed; the expression was simplified from left to right.
B. The terms of the expression were mixed up and rewritten as 3(65 + 35 + 54) = 3(154) = 462.
C. ₹170 does not include the cost of the part that needs to be replaced.

Equivalent Expressions (page 79)

77. Correct Answer: C
Apply the distributive property by multiplying the term outside the parentheses by the terms inside the parentheses: 3 times 5 and 3 times $+3r = 15 + 9r$.
Incorrect Answers:
A. *r* was omitted from the answer.
B. A multiplication error occurred: $3 \times 3 \neq 15$.
D. $+3r$ was not multiplied by 3.

78. Correct Answer: B
Apply the distributive property by multiplying the term outside the parentheses by the terms inside the parentheses: 2 times 6 and 2 times $+24k = 12 + 48k$.
Incorrect Answers:
A. 24k was not multiplied by 2.
C. 6 was not multiplied by 2.
D. *k* was omitted from the answer.

79. Correct Answer: A
Use the distributive property in reverse to factor the expression. The greatest common factor of 8 and $6x$ is 2, so divide both factors by 2 to get $2(4 + 3x)$. Check by using the distributive property.
Incorrect Answers:
B. *x* was omitted from the answer.
C. The term $4x$ was incorrectly written; the variable *x* should be omitted because there is no *x* in the first term of the original expression.
D. The terms were incorrectly added together (unlike terms cannot be added).

80. Correct Answer: D
Use the distributive property in reverse to factor the expression. The greatest common factor of $12g$ and 24 is 12, so divide both factors by 12 to get $12(g + 2)$. Check by using the distributive property.
Incorrect Answers:
A. The terms were incorrectly added together (unlike terms cannot be added).
B. *g* was omitted from the answer.
C. *g* should be included in the first term inside the parentheses instead of in the second term.

One-variable Equations and Inequalities (page 80)

81. Correct Answer: B
$(36 \div 6) + 7 = 6 + 7 = 13$
Incorrect Answers:
A. $(12 \div 6) + 7 = 2 + 7 = 9;\ 9 \neq 13$
C. $(30 \div 6) + 7 = 5 + 7 = 12;\ 12 \neq 13$
D. $(6 \div 6) + 7 = 1 + 7 = 8;\ 8 \neq 13$

82. Correct Answer: D
$3(7) - (12 \div 2) = 21 - 6 = 15;\ 15 > 10$
Incorrect Answers:
A. $3(5) - (12 \div 2) = 15 - 6 = 9;\ 9 < 10$
B. $3(3) - (12 \div 2) = 9 - 6 = 3;\ 3 < 10$
C. $3(4) - (12 \div 2) = 12 - 6 = 6;\ 6 < 10$

83. Correct Answer: A
$(12 \times 4) \div 8 = 48 \div 8 = 6$
Incorrect Answers:
B. $4 + 50 - 23 = 54 - 23 = 31;\ 31 \neq 35$
C. $(15 - 5) + 5(4) = 10 + 20 = 30$ and $6 \times 5 = 30;\ 30 = 30$
D. $8(4) + 16 = 32 + 16 = 48$ and $3 \times 14 = 42;\ 48 \neq 42$

84. Correct Answer: C
$(5 \times 7) + (64 \div 8) = 35 + 8 = 43$
Incorrect Answers:
A. $9 + 6 + 2(8) = 15 + 16 = 31;\ 31 \neq 29$
B. $46 - 8 = 38$ and $6 \times 7 = 42;\ 38 < 42$
D. $(8 - 3) + (4 \times 9) = 5 + 36 = 41$ and $58 - 12 = 46;\ 41 \neq 46$

Area (page 81)

85. Correct Answer: C
The area of the parallelogram equals the area of the rectangle:
$A = bh = 10(6) = 60$ ft.^{2}
Incorrect Answers:
A. The label *cm* is incorrect.
B. The label is incorrect; area is labeled in square units.
D. Only one half of the length of the base of the parallelogram was used to solve. The area of the triangle ($\frac{1}{2}$ bh) was found.

86. Correct Answer: D
$A = \frac{1}{2}h(b_1 + b_2) = \frac{1}{2}(18)(6 + 9) = 9(15) = 135$ cm^2
Incorrect Answers:
A. The label is incorrect; area is labeled in square units.
B. The height was not multiplied by $\frac{1}{2}$.
C. The lengths of the bases were subtracted instead of added.

87. Correct Answer: B
$A = \frac{1}{2}bh = \frac{1}{2}(6)(4) = 3(4) = 12$ m^2
Incorrect Answers:
A. The label is incorrect; area is labeled in square units.
C. The base was not multiplied by $\frac{1}{2}$.
D. The base and the height were added together (instead of multiplied) and the sum was multiplied by $\frac{1}{2}$.

88. Correct Answer: D
$A = \frac{1}{2}bh = \frac{1}{2}(22)(14) = 11(14) = 154$ in.^{2}
Incorrect Answers:
A. The label is incorrect; area is labeled in square units.
B. The base was not multiplied by $\frac{1}{2}$.
C. The base and the height were added together (instead of multiplied) and the sum was multiplied by $\frac{1}{2}$.

Explanations for Test C Answers *(cont.)*

Volume of Rectangular Prisms with Fractional Sides (page 82)

89. Correct Answer: C
$V = l \times w \times h = 8 \times 2\frac{5}{8} \times 2 = 8 \times \frac{21}{8} \times 2 = 21 \times 2 = 42$
Incorrect Answers:
A. The label is incorrect; volume is labeled in cubic units.
B. The wrong operation (addition) was used.
D. An error occurred when simplifying after multiplying $8 \times \frac{21}{8}$: $\frac{168}{8} \neq 20$.

90. Correct Answer: B
$V = l \times w \times h = 4 \times 3\frac{3}{4} \times 4 = 4 \times \frac{15}{4} \times 4 = 15 \times 4 = 60$
Incorrect Answers:
A. The wrong operation (addition) was used.
C. An error occurred when simplifying after multiplying $4 \times \frac{15}{4}$: $\frac{60}{4} \neq 12$.
D. The label is incorrect; volume is labeled in cubic units.

91. Correct Answer: A
$V = l \times w \times h = 4 \times 2\frac{1}{3} \times 4 = 3 \times \frac{7}{3} \times 4 = 7 \times 4 = 28$
Incorrect Answers:
B. An error occurred when simplifying after multiplying $4 \times \frac{7}{3}$: $\frac{28}{3} \neq 7$.
C. The wrong operation (addition) was used.
D. The label is incorrect; volume is labeled in cubic units.

92. Correct Answer: C
$V = l \times w \times h = 4 \times 2\frac{1}{4} \times 4 = 4 \times \frac{9}{4} \times 4 = 9 \times 4 = 36$
Incorrect Answers:
A. The label is incorrect; volume is labeled in cubic units.
B. The wrong operation (addition) was used.
D. An error occurred when simplifying after multiplying: $4 \times \frac{9}{4}$: $\frac{36}{4} \neq 8$.

Dot Plots (page 83)

93. Correct Answer: A
2 + 0 + 0 + 0 + 9 + 14 + 12 + 12 + 21 + 20 = 90 lions
Incorrect Answers:
B. 88 lions did not include the 2 lions observed on day 1.
C. 81 lions did not include the 9 lions observed on day 5.
D. 78 lions did not include the 12 lions observed on day 7 or on day 8.

94. Correct Answer: C
mean = (2 + 0 + 0 + 0 + 9 + 14 + 12 + 12 + 21 + 20) ÷ 10 = 90 ÷ 10 = 9 lions
Incorrect Answers:
A. 10 is the number of days Rahul and Seema were on their trip.
B. *Days* is the wrong label.
D. 21 lions is the greatest number of lions Rahul and Seema saw on one day.

95. Correct Answer: D
Order the values from least to greatest: 0, 0, 0, 2, 9, 12, 12, 14, 20, 21. Since there is an even number of data values, the median is the mean of the middle two numbers: median = (9 + 12) ÷ 2 = 21 ÷ 2 = 10.5.
Incorrect Answers:
A. A division error occurred: 21 ÷ 2 ≠ 10.
B. Since 9 and 12 are the two middle values, the median of the data is their mean.
C. The three 0 values were omitted from the list of values.

96. Correct Answer: B
On day 1 Rahul and Seema saw 2 lions; 2 is an outlier because it lies away from the other data values, which range from 9 to 21.
Incorrect Answers:
A. On Day 9 Rahul and Seema saw 21 lions; 21 is not an outlier because there is another value (20) close to it.
C. On days 7 and 8 Rahul and Seema saw 12 lions; 12 is not an outlier because there are other values close to it (9 and 14).
D. The outlier is 2 lions on Day 1.

Histograms and Box Plots (page 84)

97. Correct Answer: B
There are clusters from 20 to 49; a cluster is a range in which the greatest amount of data falls. 80 to 89 is an outlier because it is separated from the rest of the data.
Incorrect Answers:
A. There is a gap between 50 and 79, not an outlier.
C. There is an outlier from 80 to 89, but the clusters are from 20 to 49.
D. The histogram has no noticeable shape distribution.

98. Correct Answer: A
The median is the value in the middle of the box plot. To calculate the median from the list of data, find the middle value. 1, 5, 6, 7, 7, 7, 9: 7 is the median.
Incorrect Answers:
B. 6 is not the number in the middle of the list.
C. 5 is not the number in the middle of the list.
D. 9 is the greatest number in the data.

99. Correct Answer: D
Calculate the mean: mean = (1 + 5 + 6 + 7 + 7 + 8 + 9) ÷ 7 = 43 ÷ 7 = 6.1 = 6.
Then calculate the difference between the mean and each data value: 6 – 1 = *5*; 6 – 5 = *1*; 6 – 6 = *0*; 7 – 6 = *1*; 7 – 6 = *1*; 8 – 6 = *2*; 9 – 6 = *3*.
Finally, calculate the mean of the differences: mean absolute deviation = (5 + 1 + 0 + 1 + 1 + 2 + 3) ÷ 7 = 13 ÷ 7 = 1.8 = 2.
Incorrect Answers:
A. 6 is the mean.
B. 7 is the number of data values and the median.
C. 43 is the total of the data values.

100. Correct Answer: C
8 (3rd quartile) – 5 (1st quartile) = 3
Incorrect Answers:
A. 1 is the least number in the list.
B. 8 is the 3rd quartile.
D. 9 is the greatest number in the list.

Name: ______________________________ Date: __________

Bubble Answer Sheet Test A

1. Ⓐ Ⓑ Ⓒ Ⓓ	18. Ⓐ Ⓑ Ⓒ Ⓓ	35. Ⓐ Ⓑ Ⓒ Ⓓ	51. Ⓐ Ⓑ Ⓒ Ⓓ	68. Ⓐ Ⓑ Ⓒ Ⓓ	85. Ⓐ Ⓑ Ⓒ Ⓓ
2. Ⓐ Ⓑ Ⓒ Ⓓ	19. Ⓐ Ⓑ Ⓒ Ⓓ	36. Ⓐ Ⓑ Ⓒ Ⓓ	52. Ⓐ Ⓑ Ⓒ Ⓓ	69. Ⓐ Ⓑ Ⓒ Ⓓ	86. Ⓐ Ⓑ Ⓒ Ⓓ
3. Ⓐ Ⓑ Ⓒ Ⓓ	20. Ⓐ Ⓑ Ⓒ Ⓓ	37. Ⓐ Ⓑ Ⓒ Ⓓ	53. Ⓐ Ⓑ Ⓒ Ⓓ	70. Ⓐ Ⓑ Ⓒ Ⓓ	87. Ⓐ Ⓑ Ⓒ Ⓓ
4. Ⓐ Ⓑ Ⓒ Ⓓ	21. Ⓐ Ⓑ Ⓒ Ⓓ	38. Ⓐ Ⓑ Ⓒ Ⓓ	54. Ⓐ Ⓑ Ⓒ Ⓓ	71. Ⓐ Ⓑ Ⓒ Ⓓ	88. Ⓐ Ⓑ Ⓒ Ⓓ
5. Ⓐ Ⓑ Ⓒ Ⓓ	22. Ⓐ Ⓑ Ⓒ Ⓓ	39. Ⓐ Ⓑ Ⓒ Ⓓ	55. Ⓐ Ⓑ Ⓒ Ⓓ	72. Ⓐ Ⓑ Ⓒ Ⓓ	89. Ⓐ Ⓑ Ⓒ Ⓓ
6. Ⓐ Ⓑ Ⓒ Ⓓ	23. Ⓐ Ⓑ Ⓒ Ⓓ	40. Ⓐ Ⓑ Ⓒ Ⓓ	56. Ⓐ Ⓑ Ⓒ Ⓓ	73. Ⓐ Ⓑ Ⓒ Ⓓ	90. Ⓐ Ⓑ Ⓒ Ⓓ
7. Ⓐ Ⓑ Ⓒ Ⓓ	24. Ⓐ Ⓑ Ⓒ Ⓓ	41. Ⓐ Ⓑ Ⓒ Ⓓ	57. Ⓐ Ⓑ Ⓒ Ⓓ	74. Ⓐ Ⓑ Ⓒ Ⓓ	91. Ⓐ Ⓑ Ⓒ Ⓓ
8. Ⓐ Ⓑ Ⓒ Ⓓ	25. Ⓐ Ⓑ Ⓒ Ⓓ	42. Ⓐ Ⓑ Ⓒ Ⓓ	58. Ⓐ Ⓑ Ⓒ Ⓓ	75. Ⓐ Ⓑ Ⓒ Ⓓ	92. Ⓐ Ⓑ Ⓒ Ⓓ
9. Ⓐ Ⓑ Ⓒ Ⓓ	26. Ⓐ Ⓑ Ⓒ Ⓓ	43. Ⓐ Ⓑ Ⓒ Ⓓ	59. Ⓐ Ⓑ Ⓒ Ⓓ	76. Ⓐ Ⓑ Ⓒ Ⓓ	93. Ⓐ Ⓑ Ⓒ Ⓓ
10. Ⓐ Ⓑ Ⓒ Ⓓ	27. Ⓐ Ⓑ Ⓒ Ⓓ	44. Ⓐ Ⓑ Ⓒ Ⓓ	60. Ⓐ Ⓑ Ⓒ Ⓓ	77. Ⓐ Ⓑ Ⓒ Ⓓ	94. Ⓐ Ⓑ Ⓒ Ⓓ
11. Ⓐ Ⓑ Ⓒ Ⓓ	28. Ⓐ Ⓑ Ⓒ Ⓓ	45. Ⓐ Ⓑ Ⓒ Ⓓ	61. Ⓐ Ⓑ Ⓒ Ⓓ	78. Ⓐ Ⓑ Ⓒ Ⓓ	95. Ⓐ Ⓑ Ⓒ Ⓓ
12. Ⓐ Ⓑ Ⓒ Ⓓ	29. Ⓐ Ⓑ Ⓒ Ⓓ	46. Ⓐ Ⓑ Ⓒ Ⓓ	62. Ⓐ Ⓑ Ⓒ Ⓓ	79. Ⓐ Ⓑ Ⓒ Ⓓ	96. Ⓐ Ⓑ Ⓒ Ⓓ
13. Ⓐ Ⓑ Ⓒ Ⓓ	30. Ⓐ Ⓑ Ⓒ Ⓓ	47. Ⓐ Ⓑ Ⓒ Ⓓ	63. Ⓐ Ⓑ Ⓒ Ⓓ	80. Ⓐ Ⓑ Ⓒ Ⓓ	97. Ⓐ Ⓑ Ⓒ Ⓓ
14. Ⓐ Ⓑ Ⓒ Ⓓ	31. Ⓐ Ⓑ Ⓒ Ⓓ	48. Ⓐ Ⓑ Ⓒ Ⓓ	64. Ⓐ Ⓑ Ⓒ Ⓓ	81. Ⓐ Ⓑ Ⓒ Ⓓ	98. Ⓐ Ⓑ Ⓒ Ⓓ
15. Ⓐ Ⓑ Ⓒ Ⓓ	32. Ⓐ Ⓑ Ⓒ Ⓓ	49. Ⓐ Ⓑ Ⓒ Ⓓ	65. Ⓐ Ⓑ Ⓒ Ⓓ	82. Ⓐ Ⓑ Ⓒ Ⓓ	99 Ⓐ Ⓑ Ⓒ Ⓓ
16. Ⓐ Ⓑ Ⓒ Ⓓ	33. Ⓐ Ⓑ Ⓒ Ⓓ	50. Ⓐ Ⓑ Ⓒ Ⓓ	66. Ⓐ Ⓑ Ⓒ Ⓓ	83. Ⓐ Ⓑ Ⓒ Ⓓ	100. Ⓐ Ⓑ Ⓒ Ⓓ
17. Ⓐ Ⓑ Ⓒ Ⓓ	34. Ⓐ Ⓑ Ⓒ Ⓓ		67. Ⓐ Ⓑ Ⓒ Ⓓ	84. Ⓐ Ⓑ Ⓒ Ⓓ	

Name: ______________________________ **Date:** __________

Bubble Answer Sheet Test B

1. Ⓐ Ⓑ Ⓒ Ⓓ	18. Ⓐ Ⓑ Ⓒ Ⓓ	35. Ⓐ Ⓑ Ⓒ Ⓓ	51. Ⓐ Ⓑ Ⓒ Ⓓ	68. Ⓐ Ⓑ Ⓒ Ⓓ	85. Ⓐ Ⓑ Ⓒ Ⓓ
2. Ⓐ Ⓑ Ⓒ Ⓓ	19. Ⓐ Ⓑ Ⓒ Ⓓ	36. Ⓐ Ⓑ Ⓒ Ⓓ	52. Ⓐ Ⓑ Ⓒ Ⓓ	69. Ⓐ Ⓑ Ⓒ Ⓓ	86. Ⓐ Ⓑ Ⓒ Ⓓ
3. Ⓐ Ⓑ Ⓒ Ⓓ	20. Ⓐ Ⓑ Ⓒ Ⓓ	37. Ⓐ Ⓑ Ⓒ Ⓓ	53. Ⓐ Ⓑ Ⓒ Ⓓ	70. Ⓐ Ⓑ Ⓒ Ⓓ	87. Ⓐ Ⓑ Ⓒ Ⓓ
4. Ⓐ Ⓑ Ⓒ Ⓓ	21. Ⓐ Ⓑ Ⓒ Ⓓ	38. Ⓐ Ⓑ Ⓒ Ⓓ	54. Ⓐ Ⓑ Ⓒ Ⓓ	71. Ⓐ Ⓑ Ⓒ Ⓓ	88. Ⓐ Ⓑ Ⓒ Ⓓ
5. Ⓐ Ⓑ Ⓒ Ⓓ	22. Ⓐ Ⓑ Ⓒ Ⓓ	39. Ⓐ Ⓑ Ⓒ Ⓓ	55. Ⓐ Ⓑ Ⓒ Ⓓ	72. Ⓐ Ⓑ Ⓒ Ⓓ	89. Ⓐ Ⓑ Ⓒ Ⓓ
6. Ⓐ Ⓑ Ⓒ Ⓓ	23. Ⓐ Ⓑ Ⓒ Ⓓ	40. Ⓐ Ⓑ Ⓒ Ⓓ	56. Ⓐ Ⓑ Ⓒ Ⓓ	73. Ⓐ Ⓑ Ⓒ Ⓓ	90. Ⓐ Ⓑ Ⓒ Ⓓ
7. Ⓐ Ⓑ Ⓒ Ⓓ	24. Ⓐ Ⓑ Ⓒ Ⓓ	41. Ⓐ Ⓑ Ⓒ Ⓓ	57. Ⓐ Ⓑ Ⓒ Ⓓ	74. Ⓐ Ⓑ Ⓒ Ⓓ	91. Ⓐ Ⓑ Ⓒ Ⓓ
8. Ⓐ Ⓑ Ⓒ Ⓓ	25. Ⓐ Ⓑ Ⓒ Ⓓ	42. Ⓐ Ⓑ Ⓒ Ⓓ	58. Ⓐ Ⓑ Ⓒ Ⓓ	75. Ⓐ Ⓑ Ⓒ Ⓓ	92. Ⓐ Ⓑ Ⓒ Ⓓ
9. Ⓐ Ⓑ Ⓒ Ⓓ	26. Ⓐ Ⓑ Ⓒ Ⓓ	43. Ⓐ Ⓑ Ⓒ Ⓓ	59. Ⓐ Ⓑ Ⓒ Ⓓ	76. Ⓐ Ⓑ Ⓒ Ⓓ	93. Ⓐ Ⓑ Ⓒ Ⓓ
10. Ⓐ Ⓑ Ⓒ Ⓓ	27. Ⓐ Ⓑ Ⓒ Ⓓ	44. Ⓐ Ⓑ Ⓒ Ⓓ	60. Ⓐ Ⓑ Ⓒ Ⓓ	77. Ⓐ Ⓑ Ⓒ Ⓓ	94. Ⓐ Ⓑ Ⓒ Ⓓ
11. Ⓐ Ⓑ Ⓒ Ⓓ	28. Ⓐ Ⓑ Ⓒ Ⓓ	45. Ⓐ Ⓑ Ⓒ Ⓓ	61. Ⓐ Ⓑ Ⓒ Ⓓ	78. Ⓐ Ⓑ Ⓒ Ⓓ	95. Ⓐ Ⓑ Ⓒ Ⓓ
12. Ⓐ Ⓑ Ⓒ Ⓓ	29. Ⓐ Ⓑ Ⓒ Ⓓ	46. Ⓐ Ⓑ Ⓒ Ⓓ	62. Ⓐ Ⓑ Ⓒ Ⓓ	79. Ⓐ Ⓑ Ⓒ Ⓓ	96. Ⓐ Ⓑ Ⓒ Ⓓ
13. Ⓐ Ⓑ Ⓒ Ⓓ	30. Ⓐ Ⓑ Ⓒ Ⓓ	47. Ⓐ Ⓑ Ⓒ Ⓓ	63. Ⓐ Ⓑ Ⓒ Ⓓ	80. Ⓐ Ⓑ Ⓒ Ⓓ	97. Ⓐ Ⓑ Ⓒ Ⓓ
14. Ⓐ Ⓑ Ⓒ Ⓓ	31. Ⓐ Ⓑ Ⓒ Ⓓ	48. Ⓐ Ⓑ Ⓒ Ⓓ	64. Ⓐ Ⓑ Ⓒ Ⓓ	81. Ⓐ Ⓑ Ⓒ Ⓓ	98. Ⓐ Ⓑ Ⓒ Ⓓ
15. Ⓐ Ⓑ Ⓒ Ⓓ	32. Ⓐ Ⓑ Ⓒ Ⓓ	49. Ⓐ Ⓑ Ⓒ Ⓓ	65. Ⓐ Ⓑ Ⓒ Ⓓ	82. Ⓐ Ⓑ Ⓒ Ⓓ	99 Ⓐ Ⓑ Ⓒ Ⓓ
16. Ⓐ Ⓑ Ⓒ Ⓓ	33. Ⓐ Ⓑ Ⓒ Ⓓ	50. Ⓐ Ⓑ Ⓒ Ⓓ	66. Ⓐ Ⓑ Ⓒ Ⓓ	83. Ⓐ Ⓑ Ⓒ Ⓓ	100. Ⓐ Ⓑ Ⓒ Ⓓ
17. Ⓐ Ⓑ Ⓒ Ⓓ	34. Ⓐ Ⓑ Ⓒ Ⓓ		67. Ⓐ Ⓑ Ⓒ Ⓓ	84. Ⓐ Ⓑ Ⓒ Ⓓ	

Name: ______________________________ **Date:** ____________

Bubble Answer Sheet Test C

1. Ⓐ Ⓑ Ⓒ Ⓓ
2. Ⓐ Ⓑ Ⓒ Ⓓ
3. Ⓐ Ⓑ Ⓒ Ⓓ
4. Ⓐ Ⓑ Ⓒ Ⓓ
5. Ⓐ Ⓑ Ⓒ Ⓓ
6. Ⓐ Ⓑ Ⓒ Ⓓ
7. Ⓐ Ⓑ Ⓒ Ⓓ
8. Ⓐ Ⓑ Ⓒ Ⓓ
9. Ⓐ Ⓑ Ⓒ Ⓓ
10. Ⓐ Ⓑ Ⓒ Ⓓ
11. Ⓐ Ⓑ Ⓒ Ⓓ
12. Ⓐ Ⓑ Ⓒ Ⓓ
13. Ⓐ Ⓑ Ⓒ Ⓓ
14. Ⓐ Ⓑ Ⓒ Ⓓ
15. Ⓐ Ⓑ Ⓒ Ⓓ
16. Ⓐ Ⓑ Ⓒ Ⓓ
17. Ⓐ Ⓑ Ⓒ Ⓓ
18. Ⓐ Ⓑ Ⓒ Ⓓ
19. Ⓐ Ⓑ Ⓒ Ⓓ
20. Ⓐ Ⓑ Ⓒ Ⓓ
21. Ⓐ Ⓑ Ⓒ Ⓓ
22. Ⓐ Ⓑ Ⓒ Ⓓ
23. Ⓐ Ⓑ Ⓒ Ⓓ
24. Ⓐ Ⓑ Ⓒ Ⓓ
25. Ⓐ Ⓑ Ⓒ Ⓓ
26. Ⓐ Ⓑ Ⓒ Ⓓ
27. Ⓐ Ⓑ Ⓒ Ⓓ
28. Ⓐ Ⓑ Ⓒ Ⓓ
29. Ⓐ Ⓑ Ⓒ Ⓓ
30. Ⓐ Ⓑ Ⓒ Ⓓ
31. Ⓐ Ⓑ Ⓒ Ⓓ
32. Ⓐ Ⓑ Ⓒ Ⓓ
33. Ⓐ Ⓑ Ⓒ Ⓓ
34. Ⓐ Ⓑ Ⓒ Ⓓ
35. Ⓐ Ⓑ Ⓒ Ⓓ
36. Ⓐ Ⓑ Ⓒ Ⓓ
37. Ⓐ Ⓑ Ⓒ Ⓓ
38. Ⓐ Ⓑ Ⓒ Ⓓ
39. Ⓐ Ⓑ Ⓒ Ⓓ
40. Ⓐ Ⓑ Ⓒ Ⓓ
41. Ⓐ Ⓑ Ⓒ Ⓓ
42. Ⓐ Ⓑ Ⓒ Ⓓ
43. Ⓐ Ⓑ Ⓒ Ⓓ
44. Ⓐ Ⓑ Ⓒ Ⓓ
45. Ⓐ Ⓑ Ⓒ Ⓓ
46. Ⓐ Ⓑ Ⓒ Ⓓ
47. Ⓐ Ⓑ Ⓒ Ⓓ
48. Ⓐ Ⓑ Ⓒ Ⓓ
49. Ⓐ Ⓑ Ⓒ Ⓓ
50. Ⓐ Ⓑ Ⓒ Ⓓ
51. Ⓐ Ⓑ Ⓒ Ⓓ
52. Ⓐ Ⓑ Ⓒ Ⓓ
53. Ⓐ Ⓑ Ⓒ Ⓓ
54. Ⓐ Ⓑ Ⓒ Ⓓ
55. Ⓐ Ⓑ Ⓒ Ⓓ
56. Ⓐ Ⓑ Ⓒ Ⓓ
57. Ⓐ Ⓑ Ⓒ Ⓓ
58. Ⓐ Ⓑ Ⓒ Ⓓ
59. Ⓐ Ⓑ Ⓒ Ⓓ
60. Ⓐ Ⓑ Ⓒ Ⓓ
61. Ⓐ Ⓑ Ⓒ Ⓓ
62. Ⓐ Ⓑ Ⓒ Ⓓ
63. Ⓐ Ⓑ Ⓒ Ⓓ
64. Ⓐ Ⓑ Ⓒ Ⓓ
65. Ⓐ Ⓑ Ⓒ Ⓓ
66. Ⓐ Ⓑ Ⓒ Ⓓ
67. Ⓐ Ⓑ Ⓒ Ⓓ
68. Ⓐ Ⓑ Ⓒ Ⓓ
69. Ⓐ Ⓑ Ⓒ Ⓓ
70. Ⓐ Ⓑ Ⓒ Ⓓ
71. Ⓐ Ⓑ Ⓒ Ⓓ
72. Ⓐ Ⓑ Ⓒ Ⓓ
73. Ⓐ Ⓑ Ⓒ Ⓓ
74. Ⓐ Ⓑ Ⓒ Ⓓ
75. Ⓐ Ⓑ Ⓒ Ⓓ
76. Ⓐ Ⓑ Ⓒ Ⓓ
77. Ⓐ Ⓑ Ⓒ Ⓓ
78. Ⓐ Ⓑ Ⓒ Ⓓ
79. Ⓐ Ⓑ Ⓒ Ⓓ
80. Ⓐ Ⓑ Ⓒ Ⓓ
81. Ⓐ Ⓑ Ⓒ Ⓓ
82. Ⓐ Ⓑ Ⓒ Ⓓ
83. Ⓐ Ⓑ Ⓒ Ⓓ
84. Ⓐ Ⓑ Ⓒ Ⓓ
85. Ⓐ Ⓑ Ⓒ Ⓓ
86. Ⓐ Ⓑ Ⓒ Ⓓ
87. Ⓐ Ⓑ Ⓒ Ⓓ
88. Ⓐ Ⓑ Ⓒ Ⓓ
89. Ⓐ Ⓑ Ⓒ Ⓓ
90. Ⓐ Ⓑ Ⓒ Ⓓ
91. Ⓐ Ⓑ Ⓒ Ⓓ
92. Ⓐ Ⓑ Ⓒ Ⓓ
93. Ⓐ Ⓑ Ⓒ Ⓓ
94. Ⓐ Ⓑ Ⓒ Ⓓ
95. Ⓐ Ⓑ Ⓒ Ⓓ
96. Ⓐ Ⓑ Ⓒ Ⓓ
97. Ⓐ Ⓑ Ⓒ Ⓓ
98. Ⓐ Ⓑ Ⓒ Ⓓ
99 Ⓐ Ⓑ Ⓒ Ⓓ
100. Ⓐ Ⓑ Ⓒ Ⓓ